SURVIVING YOUR TEENAGER

and being happy anyway

JUDITH JOY

INDIGORIVER
PUBLISHING

Surviving
Your Teenager

and being happy
anyway

JUDITH JOY

Surviving Your Teenager: And Being Happy Anyway

Copyright © 2014 by Judith Joy

Editors: Adam Tillinghast, Christian Pacheco, April Miller, Donna Melillo
Cover Design: Jason Kauffmann / Firelight Interactive / firelightinteractive.com
Cover Illustration: Arkie Ring
Interior Design: Rick Soldin / book-comp.com

Indigo River Publishing
3 West Garden Street Ste. 352
Pensacola, FL 32502
www.indigoriverpublishing.com

Ordering Information:
Quantity sales: Special discounts are available on quantity purchases by corporations, associations, and others. For details, contact the publisher at the address above.

Orders by U.S. trade bookstores and wholesalers: Please contact the publisher at the address above.

Printed in the United States of America

Publisher's Cataloging-in-Publication Data is available upon request.

Library of Congress Control Number: 2013958056

ISBN 978-0-9860493-1-6

First Edition

*With Indigo River Publishing, you can always expect great books,
strong voices, and meaningful messages.
Most importantly, you'll always find ... words worth reading.*

This book is dedicated to my mother, Audrey Miller, an example of unconditional love. You always believed in me and I know that you are smiling down from heaven, continuing to send your love and guidance. I hope to share this love with others and share the joy it brings.

Contents

Appendix

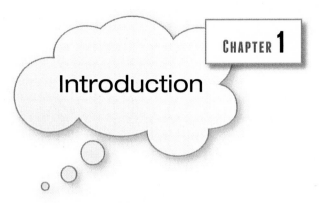

Introduction

It's Possible to be Happy
(And Still Have a Teenager)

My intuition was awake at one in the morning; the same time my almost-17-year-old son, Adam, opened my bedroom door and said, "I don't feel well. My throat hurts, and I sweat so much my sheets are wet." After he climbed into bed for a snuggle, I asked my intuition what this was about. I heard, "Alcohol." Interesting. So, I asked my son if he'd been drinking at prom the previous night. He hemmed and hawed, then admitted that they had done some but wouldn't admit to how much. (Telling the truth is a HUGE deal for me, and the kids know that if they lie, the punishment will be MUCH worse.)

As it turned out, the sweating only lasted that night. The sore throat, headache, and body aches lasted a few days. This made it look like he was sick, so I let him stay at home and miss school.

My intuition was telling me what the problem was, but my conscious mind got in the way and thought it was an illness ... until my older son told me that drinking too much can cause body sweats. My response was, "Interesting." I then went to Adam's room and calmly said, "I just found out that alcohol causes body sweats. I'll bet that is what you were experiencing. If I'd known that, I would have made you go to school even though you didn't feel well. Consider yourself warned if you try it again. If you play, you pay—and by the way, if it takes you four days to feel good after drinking, you may not want to do it anymore. Now I'll have to think of a punishment." I then walked out. Being sick on top of a hangover can work to my advantage. His body will remember the connection.

Wow, had my parenting changed! I listened to my intuition and trusted what showed up. No threats. No yelling. No long lectures. I let him experience the consequences (although not all of them) and take responsibility for his actions. I also now know that he drinks, and I will increase the dialogue about that.

This change in parenting didn't happen overnight. But it did happen as I listened to myself and learned from a zillion classes, books, and teachers in order to find a way to get out of pain from daily headaches. Along that path, I learned how to be happy anyway. And that's what this book is about.

THIS IS NOT . . . I repeat . . . THIS IS NOT a book about raising your teenager. THIS IS NOT a book about changing your teenager. THIS IS NOT a book about asking or forcing other people to be different.

THIS IS a book about surviving your teenager. THIS IS a book about changing how you react to all the crazy stuff your teenager will throw in your path. THIS IS a book about letting go of the ludicrous idea that you can only be as happy as your unhappiest child. THIS IS a book about finding the joy that is already within you. THIS IS a book about looking within yourself and making the choice to be happy. THIS IS a book about choosing how you truly desire to feel. THIS IS a book that will give you the guidelines to surviving almost everything in your life. THIS IS a book that will help you find your happiness.

And this means changing you.

You are your teen's greatest teacher and role model. Be the example. Be the change. This book will help you rediscover the happy you hiding within you.

Sometimes when our children are in the throes of growing up, we get so wrapped up in the drama that we forget whom we really and truly are. Yelling, threatening, punishing, and living in turmoil become the norm … but it doesn't have to be that way. We can be loving, supportive, encouraging, AND still hold the boundaries that are so important while feeling calm and peaceful on the inside.

Please know that this is possible, even if you read no further. There is another way … if you change your perspective.

Why should you listen to me? I've lived through it and have gone from depression to happiness (without pharmaceuticals, although I tried that route too). Sure my four kids have grown up and the pressure isn't the same, but I'm not the same either—and I've learned some things along the way. With one teenager still at home, I see that my parenting has changed because I have changed. I used to be punishment-oriented and very stuck in my ways with what was the "right" thing to do.

I've opened up to the idea that while my way may be "a" right way, it isn't the only one. Now I'm much more likely to look at what they do and comment something like, "That's an interesting choice." In addition, I'm better at listening to my children. It's easier to see what their true desires are and allow them to follow them without putting a negative spin (my old perspective) on their choices.

The biggest change is within me. I'm happier; I'm listening to myself; I'm standing up for myself; I'm being honest with me. And if I can do this for myself, it allows me the space to do it with my children too.

It's a matter of perspective. If you change the way you look at something, it can become different—and all you did was look at it in a new way.

When I began on this road to happiness, joy, and peace, it was to get rid of pain from my daily headaches. I didn't even know that happiness was the goal. I just knew that I wanted to feel better. I started in western medicine, but that didn't work. So, I looked into the alternative therapies, where I found a home.

I approached it as I usually do. I asked questions, took classes, read a lot, and found a mentor (Dr. Ron Jahner, a truly gifted naturopathic physician). I followed my interests; and along the way, I was guided to my new perspective. In fact, my father even said, "I have no idea what you are doing, but keep doing it. You are much happier and more at peace."

This book is a compilation of what I've learned and what has helped me. I've tried not to copy anyone else's work. If I've inadvertently done this, I apologize. While a specific program or author may do a better job of explaining something, I've noticed that the underlying themes within many of the consciousness programs and energy transformation systems are the same. Consciousness programs clear out the garbage in the mind and increase one's awareness of the possibilities by helping uncover what is in the subconscious mind (the part we aren't aware of). Energy transformation systems help the individual shift his energy to remove the limitations and disabilities within himself to create new possibilities. They are very similar.

At the end of the book, I've included the programs, books, DVDs, etc. that have helped me, along with a commentary about some of them. I encourage you to not automatically accept what is written here. Test it out for yourself. Take the programs, read the books, and watch the DVDs. Discover your own truths.

Possibilities of Something New

I know you are busy and just want to get to it, so let's begin. Everything is a possibility—an opening to something new. This includes all the stupid stuff that our teenagers do.

Oh? Your child is perfect and never does anything stupid? Terrific! But I'll bet that your child is a human being; and no matter how good he is, stupid stuff happens some of the time. And if you don't like the word "stupid", think of it as an unfortunate turn of events. Or think of it as a learning experience. Or think of it as growing pains. Or think of it as a new and interesting way to deal with an issue. Or think of it as something that will help him become a more loving and compassionate human being.

Already, all we have done is change how we think of the "stupid" stuff. We didn't change anything except our viewpoint—our perspective—and in doing so, we feel better. We started at a low-feeling viewpoint and ended up at a hopeful perspective that feels good. If you do this often enough, (another way to say practice) then it becomes automatic.

Now imagine the next time your teenager is "discovered" doing something in a "new and interesting way that you wouldn't think of doing but you know will lead to him being more compassionate" (remember, you've been practicing changing your perspective), the way you respond will be different. And since this response is new (and calmer), the whole situation has an opportunity to shift and be different.

Can it be even better than this? Yes. And can it be even better than that? Yes. And even better than that? Yes, it can! But keep your options open. Allow for the possibility that it can be even better than that. The better you feel, the better it gets.

CHAPTER 1
Consciousness Concept Review

Happiness/Expanding Your Perspective

▶ It's possible to be happy.

▶ It's possible to rediscover the happy you that is already there.

▶ You can change your perspective.

▶ Changing your perspective changes how you feel.

▶ You are the only person you can change directly.

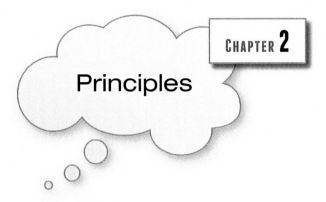

Principles

Who is Living Your Life?

Remember how your teenager keeps telling you to back off when you try to lay down the law? He always tells you to stop telling him what to do—that it's his life and his choice to make. He can do it on his own. Those teens have a certain point. (In an ideal world, I wouldn't have to choose "him" or "her," but for simplicity, I will continue to use the masculine term.)

Who is living your life? You are. And as such, you get to decide what you think, feel, and do. Too many people are afraid to be different from who they were told they are. This doesn't mean that what they were told is correct. It's just someone's opinion. Somewhere along the way, people just accept what others have said as being true and as such, live up to others' expectations.

But what about your own expectations? Have you fulfilled them? Do you even know what they are? What is it that you really desire underneath it all? What feeling are you looking for?

Now, it's time for you to make a decision. Do you hope to stay the same, or do you wish for something different? If you choose to stay the same, thank you for reading this far, but you can put the book down now. If you choose to continue reading, I'm warning you that your mind will expand. Different thoughts create a new reality.

If you chose something different, *woo hoo!* Thanks for joining me on this journey. It's going to be exciting and fun as we rediscover who you really are.

How the Universe Works

The ultimate objective of your life is to be you—who you *really* are. You need the freedom within yourself to do this.

The Universe has a force or energy to allow all the possibilities to come to you. It's there whether you are aware of it or not. Think about a cloudy day. The sun is blocked, and all you see are the clouds. The sun never went away. It's still there. The only thing that changed is your awareness of the sun. The clue is to change your perspective—your awareness—so that you harness the power to work for you instead of against you. Yes, this is possible.

So what is this force? It appears to be the background energy or matrix from which the entire Universe is continually created. It's what we and everything else are made of. Therefore, the more in harmony with that essential energy you can be, the more successful your life will become.

It's an energy that carries out your wishes, desires, intentions, expectations, and more. It's an energy that knows the real you—the you that is buried underneath all the garbage that you have been conditioned with throughout your lifetime. It's the power that is directed by your heart. It's something bigger than you. Think of it as the "work force" that makes your life run.

It's always there, quietly working and playing in the background. The great idea you just had? It's a result of the energy working with you. On some level, you set an intention to "discover" the idea. The energy took your intention and brought the idea to you ... or more accurately, to your awareness. It helps you solve the problem you were working on. It brings the people into your life to help you in some way. It moves the chess pieces of your life to help you, even if you didn't know you asked for the help.

How does the Force work? Think about an intention, expectation, goal, purpose, problem, or even a prayer, then drop into your heart and be quiet as you wait and listen. You may hear, see, feel, or in some way become aware of the answer in a minute, a day, or longer, but the Force will be working on your topic while you are going about your life taking the positive actions that will help you reach your desires.

When you do this asking, please, please, please drop the word "not." Ask for what it is you truly do desire. Change your perspective and state it in a positive way. After all, what you focus on is what you get.

The answer will show up. But will you be aware of it? You see, the world is a mirror of what you are thinking and feeling on the inside, especially feeling. What you feel is what you attract. Have you ever noticed that when you are grumpy, there are plenty of people and events around that reinforce that feeling? But when you are happy, the grumpy people seem to disappear, and happy experiences abound.

So pay attention to the signs you see in your life. They may have always been there, but your awareness of them gives you the answers you seek. Look at the experiences you are having, the people you are attracting, and the things you are noticing such as signs, books, songs, overheard conversations, random thoughts, and more. Be aware.

If you like what you are getting in your life, then keep on feeling the same way. If you don't like what you are getting, then change your feelings and the thoughts that are triggering those feelings. This will lead to new perspectives and a life more in tune with what you do desire.

There are many different names for this energy. Some people call it the Energy Field, and others call it the Universe, Light, Spirit, or even God. While I believe in God, the term is sensitive and has an emotional charge for many people; so in an effort not to offend anyone, I'll be using the terms Energy and Universe. But whatever it is called, it is a force that helps things happen. Think of it as a team member. As part of your team (everything and everyone helping you achieve your dreams), are you allowing each part of the team to work for you? Are you harnessing the power that is waiting to help you?

Ten Underlying Principles

Before we really get into it, I'd like to give you a quick (and I do mean quick) overview of some of the concepts or principles that are basic to how things work in the Universe. There are of course many more principles out there, but these are the ones that we will touch on in this book. As you read the book, you'll understand them further.

Decision Making: We each have the ability to make decisions. Whether we do or don't is up to us. Whether it's hard or easy is up to us, but the ability to make decisions is there.

Choice: When you make a decision, you are choosing between options. You can make a choice. When it feels like you don't have a choice, it's just that you don't like the options. But you do have the ability to make a choice. Of course, every choice you make puts you on a path with certain consequences. But you can make a decision and make a different choice.

Personal Responsibility: Everything in your life is your personal responsibility. You are the one choosing (even if it's just a feeling). If you're not willing to take responsibility for every-thing in your life ... and I do mean *everything* ... then put the book down and don't read it. Everything else in the book is making the assumption that YOU are taking responsibility for everything in your own life.

Feelings: Feelings are our guiding light. We aren't always aware of what we are feeling in the moment, because many of these feelings are memorized patterns (habits) that we keep feeling over and over. Our bodies "know" which of the feelings are "true." So when our thoughts say one thing and our feelings say another, the Universe defaults to the feelings, and that's what you attract. The clue is to take emotional charges off of the feelings so that you can be more proactive instead of reactive.

Vibrations: Everything vibrates—things, words, and even feelings. Vibrations either attract or repel. If the vibrations are alike, then they attract; and if they are different, they repel.

Habits: We form habits when we do something over and over. Sometimes the habits are good, and other times they can be better. But the more you do something, the more it becomes a habit. And the longer you do it, the stronger the habit becomes and the seemingly harder it is to change it.

Mirror Image: The world is a mirror. What you see around you is what you are thinking and feeling on the inside. Here's the thing: because we attract what we think and feel, we attract things, experiences, items, etc. into our lives. We each attract our "reality."

Truth: When you believe something, you think it is true, and you create your life around this truth. You trust that what you believe to be true is in fact true. However, "*It's only true until it's*

not." We only think something is true; and because we *think* it
to be true, it is ... until our thoughts change. Then a new truth
is born.

Reality: Reality is only a reality based upon your perception as
seen through the rules you live your life by. Reality is what is
true for each of us. Some people go through life and think it's
great. Others think life is hard, horrible, and an overall difficult experience. If reality was the same for everyone, people
couldn't have these different experiences.

Love and Peace: It's all about love, and love leads to peace.
When you live with the feeling of love and are truly vibrating at
this high level, life is easier.

I didn't always believe this stuff, but that doesn't mean it
wasn't there—just that I couldn't recognize it or didn't know
about it ... yet. Think of these principles as just the way it is.
There's nothing you can do about them. They operate if you
agree with them or not. The clue is to align your inner self so
that they work for you instead of against you.

CHAPTER 2
Consciousness Concept Review

Ten Underlying Principles

▶ You are the one living your life.

▶ The ultimate objective of your life is to be the real you.

▶ The energy is always there and you are using it, whether you know it or not.

▶ Ask for what you truly desire. Drop the word not.

▶ **Ten underlying principles** (Only a few of all the principles out there).

> We each have the ability to make decisions.

> You do have the ability to make a choice.

> Everything in your life is your personal responsibility.

> Feelings are your guiding light.

> Everything vibrates and either attracts similar vibrations or repels dissimilar vibrations.

> The more you do something, the more it becomes a habit.

> What you see around you is what you are thinking and feeling on the inside.

> It's only true until it's not.

> Reality is only a reality based upon your perception.

> When you live with the feeling of love, life is easier.

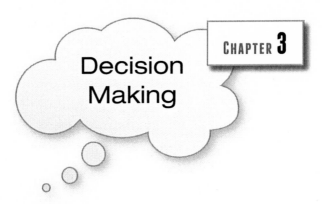

Decision Making

Your Desires are a Decision Away

The ability to make a decision is within each one of us. What we do with that ability is determined by the individual. For some people, this is difficult, while for others it's easy. But in the end, you make a decision. However, it's important to remember that when you avoid making a decision, you are in fact making one.

What can help you decide more easily? You need to know where you are going and for what purpose. This is also known as setting a goal or objective. But wait—this is a book about being happy. How does setting a goal apply?

Very simply: if you know what your overall goals or objectives are for yourself and your children, this will help guide you so that each decision can be supportive and lead you on the path to accomplishing what you set out to do. However, if you never decide what you truly desire, anything will be good enough.

If giving your children opportunities is important, then you make choices based on this objective. For example, you may choose to live in a certain neighborhood or send your children to a specific school. You may have lots of books, access to computers, and make visits to the library. You may hire tutors or encourage your children to try many extracurricular activities.

You may travel with them and give them new experiences. But if you didn't have this goal, none of these things may happen.

If you don't have the objective, then anything you do will be good enough. And every time life presents you with an opportunity, you will have to decide if it's right for you. If the objective is to give your children opportunities, then it's logical that you would encourage your children to try new things. However, if your objective was to get through the year and pass the grade, then trying new things may not be important. But if you didn't know what your objective was, then you wouldn't know if the new opportunity was right for your children or yourself. Life is much simpler if you set the goal or objective and move toward it.

I'm hearing you say, "But my kid is a teenager already. It's too late. My kid is almost grown and out of the house. This should have taken place when he was a toddler." It's never too late. At any point in time, you can make a different decision.

And the same is true for your teenager. The teen years are when he will experiment with what you have taught him. Please give him the space to make the decisions, set his own goals, and make a few mistakes. Trust that with your guidance, he will make the right choices for himself. Then when he makes choices, be there to ask, "How is that working for you?"

This simple question takes the pressure off you. It puts the responsibility back on him, where it belongs. After all, it is his life; and at some point, he hopefully will be living independently of you. If you help him make these decisions, life will be easier for everyone concerned.

So, let's look at your life. How's it working for you? Do you like your life? Do you want to make a different decision? Do you want to revamp everything or just a small part? It's your choice. Let's start from where you are in this moment. To do so, try this exercise.

PERSONAL EVALUATION EXERCISE[1]

How to do it:

1. Fold a piece of paper down the middle. On the left side, write "Doesn't Work for Me." And on the right side, write "Works for Me."
2. On the left, write all the ways your life is *not* working for you.
3. On the right, write all the ways your life *is* working for you.
4. Go back and forth as you think of different things.

REM:

Repetition: Keep writing until you are all out of ideas. Then in a few days, do the list again, as more ideas will continue to surface.

Emotion: The more honest you are with your feelings, the better the outcome will be. You are the only one who will be seeing this list. Be honest with yourself.

Motion: The act of writing takes it out of your head and gives you a place to store the information. It also frees up your mind to allow more ideas to bubble up.

Purpose:

By taking a moment and writing down the ways your life is working for you and not working for you, you can more easily see where something can be different.

---

[1] Each chapter will include at least one exercise. Additional exercises are included in Appendix A entitled "**Internal Workout Space**." Keep in mind that all the exercises are really just a way to focus on an intention. If you repeat the exercises with feeling, you will create or condition new patterns that are more beneficial for you.

Everything is Working for You

Let's look at your list. Everything is working for you in some way, or else it wouldn't be in your life. Yes, even the stuff that seems "bad" is working for you—it is supporting you in some way. For example, are you yelling at your teenager too much? How can this benefit you? Is this the only time you interact with your child? Is this what feels comfortable because it's what your parents did? Does yelling give you a feeling of superiority? In each question, you can see how yelling would help you achieve a goal that you didn't even know you had (the goal of feeling connection, comfort, or superiority).

If it weren't benefiting you somehow, you'd drop it. So, the clue is to focus on finding what you desire, what supports that desire, and then take the action steps to help you achieve it.

It's the same for all of us. What we are truly after is a feeling. Anything we do is because it will give us a feeling, and most people are in search of things that feel good. On some level, even the stuff we have or do but don't like feels good, just like the yelling might give the feeling of connection, comfort, or superiority. Often, we aren't consciously aware of what we truly desire—the real feeling we are going after. Once we identify the feeling, we can allow the Universe to bring it to us in many possible ways.

You see, all our feelings have energy attached to them. It's usually this energy that charges the experience and directs us to take specific actions, which lead to certain results. If we can neutralize the charge and change the energy, then the actions we choose will most likely be different, and thus the result will be different.

Most people start with the thought, which leads to an instant feeling about that thought. From there, they take an action and then evaluate if the action gave them the result they thought they wanted. If so, they keep doing it. If not, they go back to the thought and try to change it.

But very often until the feelings are neutralized and balanced, as you'll learn how to do later in the book, people will keep picking thoughts with similar feelings, because that is what they are used to feeling. Being comfortable feels good.

Let's use the example of a teenager experimenting with pot. (I'm making the assumption that the parents don't like this and don't smoke pot themselves.)

For the first example, the parents' thoughts could be along the lines of, "This is wrong. It's illegal. He's going to ruin his whole life. What will others think? He's throwing his life away. I have to do something, but don't know what to do." And so on.

Behind or underneath the thoughts are fear, anxiety, desperation, and possibly embarrassment. The actions these parents choose will be a result of these feelings, more so than the actual thoughts. The teen will respond to the feelings, which will help determine the direction of the conversation and eventual outcome, which probably involves a lot of yelling and threatening as well as a big punishment. But the feelings leading to the action started with the parents, even though the initial feeling-action chain started with the teen.

Now, let's say another teenager is in the same situation. However, the parents have different feelings. (I'm still assuming they don't like it and don't smoke pot.) They discover their teen smoking pot and are angry. They choose to separate themselves from their teen until they calm down. The teen is sent to his room, and the parents do something to neutralize any feelings they may have. In half an hour, they come back and say, "Alright. What's this about?" Then they listen.

In the end, the teen feels heard, the parents are truly present, and the punishment is accepted. The teen takes personal responsibility for his choices, and the parents are able to help the teen navigate the real reason he's smoking pot ... possibly to fit in with his friends, depression, loneliness, anxiety from too much pressure, etc.

In both cases, the teen is punished in some way. He didn't escape the consequences for his actions. However, once the parents in the second example were able to be peaceful and loving, they could help the teen truly solve the problem. After all, the root cause of the problem wasn't really the pot. It was just a symptom. The real problem was the feeling the teen had that led him to this action (smoking pot). And once you know what the real problem is, you can take actions to deal with it.

The Possibility Chain:
Stimulus – Perception – Belief – Thought – Feeling – Action – Review

Here's a quick overview of how this chain reaction flows. We are born with a certain temperament (usually happiness and love). As we grow, we interact with our environment, which includes parents, teachers, clergy, advertisements, friends, books, movies, songs, personal experiences, etc. Everything we are exposed to is a stimulus, a sensory experience, and creates an opportunity to form a perception.

In other words, something happens in your life experience. From this you have a perception of the event, which is your interpretation of what is around you—your point of view. You may or may not be conscious of the perception. And it can happen faster than the blink of an eye.

From the perception, you build a belief, however limiting it is, to support that interpretation. These beliefs can be very deep and widespread covering many areas of your life. They can even be tied to the belief that if you give it up, you will die. Many people hold onto their beliefs as if their lives depended upon them to do so. When in reality, a belief is just a point of view. It's not necessarily true; we just think it is.

After perception and belief, a thought is formed; and almost immediately, you have a feeling about that thought. This feeling is the motivator. It is because of this feeling that you choose the action you do.

Once you have done the action, the world reacts. The next step is to reevaluate. It's time to ask yourself, "Is this working for me?" Do you like the reaction you received? If you do, then keep doing what you are doing. After all, if you keep doing the same thing, you will keep getting the same results. However, very often people get caught up in proving that their perceptions, beliefs, thoughts, feelings, and actions are right, even though they no longer work for them. If the results of your action aren't giving you the results you desire, then go back to the beginning and tweak it.

Most people think it's the action that has to change. However, consciousness programs and energy transformation systems focus on changing a different part of the chain. All programs focus on allowing new possibilities, whether it's the beliefs, thoughts, or feelings. I've found if you change (neutralize) the emotional charge of the feeling, all the rest is easy to change. It's all about changing how you react, which entails changing how you handle your feelings. That's the whole process in a nutshell.

Begin with some questions: If it was possible to perceive, believe, think and feel something different, could you allow it? Could you let go of all your past perceptions, beliefs, thoughts, and feelings?[2] Could you? Would you? When?[3] I like to call this possibility thinking.

Chances are these questions brought up a feeling within you. You could be asking, "Do you mean that I have to let go of everything?" You could see it that way. But another way to look at it is as if you are cleaning yourself out so you can allow something even better to come in. *If you clean out the old, the new will have space to move in, and the next right action will pop up without you having to worry about it. This makes life easy.*

After you are willing to open the space within you, ask for what you *do* desire; and since we do things for the feelings they give us, "What feeling do you desire?" Put your energy and focus on this feeling. This is what you are going after, so you may as well focus here.

The key is to focus on the feeling, take the emotional charge off it, and allow something different . . . thus, how you react will change. In the end, you are looking to feel better and react to the situations in your life in a better way.

Now imagine how different your life could be if you could allow this new possibility. If you aren't carrying the weight of all the emotional charges, you open yourself to living the magical, happy life you were born to live. Life will become easy as your reaction to everything is neutralized, and the next right action leading to the fulfillment of your intentions is laid in your path. It's that easy.

---

[2] All the programs have questions. These particular questions are based on Access Consciousness. Check out this program for great questions.

[3] This question is from Lester Levinson, Release Technique.

CHAPTER 3
Consciousness Concept Review

· ·

Objectives/Everything is Working for You/ Possibility Chain

▶ Everything is working for you in some way, or else it wouldn't be in your life.

▶ Anything we do is because it will give us a feeling.

▶ All our feelings have an energy attached to them that charges the experience and directs us to take specific actions, which lead to certain results.

▶ We get to choose our thoughts.

▶ We can change our feelings.

▶ The Possibility Chain consists of stimulus – perception – belief – thought – feeling – action – review.

· ·

Intention

Being Purposeful

Everything we do has a purpose—even if we aren't consciously aware of the purpose. Setting an intention is being purposeful. When we know what it is we truly desire to accomplish, our focus brings us into the moment, the task is easier, and other possibilities to achieve the purpose come into our awareness. And as an added bonus, we know when we have succeeded. We know when the purpose has been accomplished.

Keep your attention on your intention. You will get what you focus on, so you may as well focus on what you are doing in the moment. The past is already done, and the future is decided by what you are doing in this moment. In reality, time is a series of moments. Pay attention to the moment you are in. And if you are working toward an objective, feel now how you will feel when the objective is accomplished. This keeps you focused on the feeling and in the present moment.

By being purposeful, you get rid of the clutter in your mind; and as things are clearer, they become easier.

When you know what it is you truly desire to accomplish, the Universe will move mountains to help you achieve the intentions. Additional possibilities will pop up in your consciousness, and very often they will be even better ways of achieving the true intention you are striving for. The Universe is on your team, so put it to work for you. Let it know what you truly intend and then set it free to find it.

Knowing the Purpose

Think of the Universe as a restaurant. If you give the waiter the order, he knows what to bring you. However, if you are wishy-washy, he doesn't know what you chose. A clear, concise order (intention) makes it easier for the waiter (Universe) to give you what you desire.

An intention is based in knowing the purpose you are doing something. There are three layers of intention.

- ▶ **Specific:** You know what you desire and can go after it. You are, in effect, putting blinders on and not paying attention to other opportunities. This limits the possibilities, but may be perfect for what you need.

- ▶ **Overall:** Take a step back and look at the broader purpose. This allows even better opportunities to show up, and the outcome may be different than with a specific intention.

- ▶ **Feeling:** Take a step within and look for the feeling you truly desire. Then let go and allow the Universe to bring you great opportunities.

Setting your intentions helps you by identifying what you truly hope to accomplish. Your intentions do have an effect on the outcome. As with any intention, the next right step or action is up to you. The Universe brings you the opportunity. It's up to you to do something with it.

Let's take the idea of brushing our teeth. There are many reasons we brush our teeth. Mom told us to brush every morning and evening, or after every meal. We want to please her, so we do it. We want white teeth. We want fresh breath. We want to be close to people; and if we don't brush, then people back away from our bad breath. We don't want cavities. (Remember about the word "not"? What will the Universe give us if we are focused on *not* wanting cavities? Cavities.) Let's go on. We want strong teeth. We want to be able to use our own teeth to eat corn on the cob when we are 100 years old. We want to *have* teeth when we are 100.

Or in the moment, your intention can be more focused. Perhaps you were out partying, had too much to drink, and had your drinks come up for a return visit, if you get my drift. Your intention, in this case, may be to take the horrible taste out of your mouth. Even if you don't state an intention, it's there. Of course, in more-sober moments, it is easier to recognize.

Uncover your true intention, and the action that you choose may be different, affecting the results. If your intention is clean breath, then you can use mouthwash and call it a day, or you can brush your teeth quickly. However, if your intention is to have healthy, white teeth, then you are more likely to brush your teeth for two minutes, floss, and possibly repeat this multiple times during the day. You will pay more attention to the toothpaste you use. You may even choose to eat food that is healthy for strong teeth, give up things that stain the teeth, or brush immediately after consuming them.

I purposefully chose brushing teeth because so many of us do it without really thinking. Unfortunately, we do the same— forget to be purposeful—when we do most other things.

Just as a quick aside, if you set an intention before going to bed, then the Universe can begin pulling together whatever needs to get done. So when you wake up, things are already in motion.

Truth Barometer

Which intentions feel right for you? Is there a better one? Go with the one that feels right. When you say it, you know that it's the one. Pay attention to your gut feeling, as your gut is your truth barometer. What's true feels light and expansive, and it opens you up. What's false feels heavy and constrictive. Your insides feel like they are folding in on themselves. Each consciousness system has its own way to help you determine what makes you strong and shows you your truth versus what makes you weak and is false for you. But they are all the same in the sense that you listen to what your body is telling you.

CHAPTER 4
Consciousness Concept Review:
Intentions/Being Purposeful

▶ An intention is based in knowing the purpose you are doing something. Setting an intention is being purposeful.

▶ Intentions are looking at something specific, looking at the big picture (overall), or looking within (feelings).

▶ Everything we do has a purpose behind it . . . even if we aren't consciously aware of the purpose.

▶ What you focus on is what you get.

▶ Use your truth barometer to listen to what your body is telling you.

Intention Exercise

How to do it:

1. Examine what you are about to do.
2. Determine the reasons you are doing it.
3. Keep looking for reasons until you get that "ah ha" feeling and know this is the true reason.
4. Do the activity.

REM:

Repetition: Ideally, look for your intention before you do everything.

Emotion: Pay attention to how you feel when you discover or think of the intention. Look for the emotion that feels right. This is gut instinct.

Motion: There doesn't have to be motion with this one. However, if you write down the intentions, they do become stronger ... and you are better able to remember them.

Purpose:

If you set your intention, then you are letting yourself and the Universe know what it is that you truly hope will happen. The Universe can then help you by bringing additional experiences into your life that will help you achieve your intention.

Expectations

You Get What You Expect

Now that you have set your intentions, what are you expecting? You see, you get what you expect. It's more than what you say you desire. What you truly expect in your heart (your feeling about the intention) is what you attract.

Very often, our expectations don't match up with reality, but we can't see what is truly happening because we expect something else. When Shoshanna, my daughter, came out of a residential treatment center for depression and anxiety for the second time at age 16, I intellectually knew that she was better. But on a deeper level, I expected her to behave as she had before. I was expecting the yelling, screaming, door slamming, etc. that had ruled her life before treatment. (She didn't have the hide-the-emotions, shut-down type of depression and anxiety. She was in a full-rage all the time.)

Since she was little, I knew something was "wrong" and had been taking her to doctors to "fix" it. After treatment, I still expected her to behave the same way because for years, she had been verbally abusive toward me. I was the one that had trouble letting go of the behavior, because I was frightened it might come back. So I was always on guard waiting for it and thus missed many of the improvements she had made. My focus was

31

on what I expected, and that was all I could see. It wasn't until I stepped back and adjusted my expectations (by looking for the good) that I could see she was making progress.

When I got to the point that I gave up and let her live her life as she wanted, things shifted in my mind. I just accepted her as she is instead of trying to change her. Now, I can see that she is a great, young lady walking a different path than others her age. She is happy, her self-esteem is solid, and she likes her body image. A portion of this is because we spent a summer doing the exercises in this book. We took the progress that she had made and improved upon it. She'd made the decision to be happy. I just helped her get there, but only after I changed my own expectations.

What Else Is Possible?

Are you willing to give up your old expectations to allow something new? Are you limiting yourself by holding onto your expectations? Or are you allowing new possibilities?

A quick way to open yourself up is to ask, "What else is possible?" Just asking the question is enough. You don't have to know the answers; the Universe will bring the answers to you. All you have to do is pay attention to what shows up in your life. Be open to the possibility that what shows up may be better than you expected.

What if all things are possible? What is the feeling you truly desire? What if you are pushing away possibilities by holding onto the "old" way of thinking and feeling? What if all you had to do was figure out what it is you truly desire, ask the Universe to bring it to you, and then step out of the way? What if the Universe was guiding you and telling you how to achieve your hopes and wishes and you just followed the guidance?

Once I asked what else is possible (about Shoshanna and her yelling), the Universe gave me the following: Her choice was to live in the basement of her boyfriend's grandmother's house and to help him take care of his grandmother, who has dementia. (This was an opportunity that I couldn't have provided her.) Her choice was to leave college. Her choice was to babysit (which she *loves*). Her choice is to write a novel, but only after a year of reading a book a day. Her choice was to discover what she loves ... romance, mystery, 19th century history, mythology, time travel, and more. My choice was to cut off her allowance to give her motivation to do something besides read.

And the really cool part is that I'm totally fine with all these decisions. I let go of the judgment that they are in any way good or bad. After all, judgment closes off options and limits possibilities.

I can let her be herself. She's doing what she loves. She's happy. She's mostly supporting herself. She is slowly finding herself. The benefit for me is that we have a great relationship, and she barely yells any more. She is a pleasure to be with.

I wonder what else is possible. Can it get better than that? It's going to be exciting to watch her blossom and develop further.

Expect It

If you don't want to start with letting go of your expectations (as I did above), then take the time to determine exactly what you expect to happen. Expect it. And then step out of the way to allow it to happen.

That little space between the last two sentences is the part that trips most of us up. It's just a knowingness that it will happen. This is also known as faith. The more times you allow it and see that it does work for you, the easier it is to have the faith that it will happen. It's scary at first; but when you get to the calm feeling, the sense of knowing, you are really in the moment of faith. You just know it to be so.

I can hear you now. "What are you talking about? Things don't always go as I expect." Well, let me tell you. They do.

There are two kinds of expecting. The first kind is when we think something and expect what we think to come true. This is equivalent to thinking that your teen will talk respectfully.

The second is when we feel something. For example, when your teen mouths off, you feel anger, sadness, or embarrassment. Chances are the behavior was there before, and you had the feeling before. So you know it's coming, and you have the feeling almost before it happens, which actually pulls in the behavior.

We aren't always aware of what we are feeling in the moment, because many of these feelings are memorized patterns that we keep feeling over and over. Our bodies "know" that the feelings are supposedly "true." So, when our thoughts say one thing and our feelings say another, the Universe defaults to the feelings, and that's what you get.

Now go to a time when you *didn't* get what you expected. What was your mind saying? What were your feelings saying? Were they in agreement?

Jot down your thoughts and feelings below . . .

_____

_____

_____

_____

_____

_____

Dealing with Unmet Expectations

How do you feel after reading the last section? If you are like most people, it threw you for a loop ... on an emotional level. You felt something. Or if you are like I used to be, you could be shut down and not recognize the feelings. You may sense that something was off, but you didn't know exactly what.

The first step is to recognize that something feels different, even if you can't identify it. Take the sensation (tightness in the chest, lump in the throat, pain in the stomach, etc.) that popped up in your body and recognize that it's there. It's more important that you recognize that you have a sensation then being able to label the sensation.

Many people go to a huge unmet expectation, and the feelings (sensations) about this just pop up. You may have been surprised that you still felt them as you thought you had dealt with them already. But if you do feel them, then they were stuffed down into your body, and the pressure from the repressed feelings is there even if you don't consciously know you are still feeling them.

So let's take a moment and process those feelings, which are the sensations (e.g. a tightness in the chest) associated with emotions (e.g. sad/happy). Feel whatever you are feeling. They are just sensations. Give yourself permission to feel whatever showed up. If it was possible, could you allow for a new feeling?

Now, let's look at those feelings. We are looking for the feelings ... not the logical answers. It's the emotions that tell us what's going on in the body (not the logic). Always allow time for the emotion or feeling to come back at you when you ask these questions. Work with the feelings.

Begin by going into a questioning mode. Asking questions allows something different to show up.

▶ What did the unmet expectation feel like? What feeling
   comes up?

▶ How many other times in your life did you feel that
   way? What's the feeling?

▶ Could you accept that you didn't get what you
   expected? What's the feeling?

▶ How does that feel? What feeling comes up?

▶ Are those feelings working for you? What feeling comes
   up?

▶ Are the feelings in agreement with your thoughts?
   What feeling comes up?

▶ Is there an element of fear, anger, or some other
   emotion that doesn't match love, joy, and peace? What
   feeling comes up?

▶ Do you want to keep the feelings you are currently
   experiencing, or would you like to let them go? What
   feeling comes up?

▶ When you feel the feeling, what sensation is your body
   giving you?

▶ Where is your focus?

▶ Are you scared to let go of the old and grab onto the new?

Feelings are just stuck energy, and they want to move. They
are there to communicate between your subconscious and conscious minds to let you know when things aren't synced up. To
allow them to move, all they need is for you to set the intention
to let them move.

▶ Could you allow the feeling to change?

▶ Could you allow it to be better?

▶ How does this feeling work to your advantage?

▶ How else is the feeling showing up in your life?

▶ What are you grateful for about this feeling?

▶ If it was possible, could you allow this feeling to move through you and leave?

▶ Are you willing to let all these feelings pop?

▶ Are you willing to neutralize them and let them go?

You can delve into the answers of the questions and find out more about yourself. Or you can just ask the questions and trust that once you have set the intention to move the feeling that the Universe will take care of it. The reason we ask multiple questions is to increase our focus on the intention and what we really do desire to happen.

Once you have asked the questions, you may choose to rewrite the memory of the experience as if you were coming from the feelings of love, joy and peace. After all, your mind doesn't know the difference between what really happened and what you think happened. And since you can change your thoughts, you can change your mind, which means you can rewrite your memory. So, how would you rewrite the experiences that trigger that emotion if you could change the emotion to one of love and peace?

A simple way to rewrite your memory and change your thoughts is to give gratitude or thanks for everything that has happened or is about to happen. The clue is to feel grateful for everything, even the small stuff. It's sort of like giving the Universe gold stars for all the good things that are in your life. And since your mind doesn't know the difference between what is real and what is imagined, if you give thanks, then the Universe will give you more things to be thankful for. The only thing you have to do is find stuff to be grateful for so that you are in alignment with the feeling of gratitude and are ready to receive more things to be grateful for.

Imagine the best. Don't worry. It will be better than that, and life will be even better.

CHAPTER 5
Consciousness Concept Review:

Expectations

▶ What you truly expect in your heart (your feeling center) is what you attract.

▶ Adjust your expectations by looking for the good, the advantage.

▶ Take the time to identify how you will recognize your desires when they show up.

▶ It's okay to feel however you feel.

▶ By asking questions, you can process your feelings and allow for something different to show up.

▶ Feelings are just stuck energy and want to move. They are there to let you know when your subconscious and conscious minds are not in agreement.

▶ Imagine the best. Life will be better.

Expectation Exercise

How to do it:

1. Ask yourself, "If I knew what to expect, what might that be?"
2. Don't worry about the answer. It will show up as a knowing, feeling, or some sense will "speak" to you.
3. Ask yourself, "If it was already done, how might it show up?"
4. The answer may show up immediately or in the near future. The more you practice this, the easier and faster this becomes.
5. Repeat either question as many times as it feels necessary.

REM:

Repetition: Ask the questions as often as you like. To get more clarity, you can ask more often.

Emotion: Being neutral and open to accepting what shows up allows the best "answers" to pop up.

Motion: This can be done while sitting, walking, running, driving ... in short, anywhere. The more movement you have, the clearer the answer will appear.

Purpose:

This exercise asks open-ended questions and allows for the Universe to give you the answer. It is especially good when you don't already know (or think you know) what the answer is.

Rules

Beliefs We Tell Ourselves

Unfortunately, many of us think that what we are feeling is "right" because that is what we are used to feeling. There is a story about a baby elephant with a rope tied around its ankle. The other end of the rope was attached to a fixed post. The baby elephant couldn't move very far because the rope and post were stronger than he was. As the elephant grew, it gave up and just accepted what it felt was its reality. By the time the elephant became an adult and was certainly stronger than the rope and post holding it, it could have pulled the whole thing out and walked away. But it had given up and just accepted that the rope was stronger. So, it did nothing and thus stayed exactly where it was.

People do the same thing with their beliefs. These beliefs are seen as reality. However, this "reality" is only one option. Yes, that's right. Reality is only a reality based upon your perception. Someone else having the same experience may have a different "reality."

Again back to the elephant. This time, three blind men are touching the elephant. The one touching the leg says an elephant is like a tree trunk. The one touching the tail says an elephant is small like a rope. And the one touching the side of the elephant "sees" it as a huge wall. Each experiences his own reality.

Our beliefs are the same. Whatever our beliefs are, we think are right. However, along the way, we have managed to pick up false beliefs. Maybe at one time they worked for us, or maybe we just unconsciously accepted the belief and agreed to it. But the important thing is to realize that many of the beliefs we live by aren't true for us. They can be true for someone else, but we can choose better beliefs.

The same is true of the rules we live by. The rules that we made up to support the beliefs (which were as a result of the perceptions we had) may no longer work for us. It's okay to make up new rules that work in your favor.

The level of emotions surrounding the experience, the number of times the experience was repeated, and the physical action that accompanied the experience helps determine how strong the belief is and possibly even what the belief was.

Rules Can Lie

These beliefs are the rules we choose to live our lives by. However, rules can lie. This lie causes the body to tense, the blood pressure to rise, and a general feeling of unease. This tension is a disagreement between our conscious mind and our subconscious mind and shows up as a physical reaction in our bodies. Unfortunately, this physical reaction very often shows up as physical ailments and diseases. It becomes stuck because the belief is stuck.

Imagine going through life afraid to cross the street. When we were toddlers, holding an adult's hand to cross the street kept us safe and was right. But as adults ourselves, do we still need to hold someone else's hand to safely cross the street? Of course not! Just because it was true at one point doesn't mean it still is; and perhaps the rules that we imprinted in our minds about that experience are no longer true. Maybe they weren't even true in that moment—we just thought they were. Either way, a child may need to hold someone's hand to cross the street, but an adult doesn't need the same rule any more.

We must change the underlying thoughts and feelings to make permanent changes in our bodies and in our lives. We can do this by changing the rules we live by. *There is a little bit of work involved and a willingness to be different, but it can be easy.* This is a rule. It could have been: *It takes a lot of hard work to change anything.* (But I don't happen to believe this one.) I've italicized rules throughout the book so that you can get used to identifying them. The more you learn about this, the easier it will be to rediscover the happy you that is hiding underneath the "you" who has been conditioned. It is really just an opportunity to do things in a different way ... if you can allow the possibility. You picked up messages and viewpoints about the world, yourself, and others, all the while "muddying up" who you were at the beginning. Think of it as being clean underneath all the mud. It's just a matter of perspective ... and requires a little washing to rediscover the clean you. (In the following exercise 'Identifying and Rewriting Rules Exercise' and Chapter 17, we will learn more about how to change your rules.)

CHAPTER 6
Consciousness Concepts Review

Rules

▶ Many of the beliefs we live our lives by aren't true for us. They can be true for someone else, but we can choose better beliefs.

▶ Rules can lie.

▶ This lie causes the body to tense, and this tension highlights a disagreement between our conscious mind and our subconscious mind. The disagreement shows up as a physical reaction in our bodies.

Identifying and Rewriting Rules Exercise

How to do it:

1. When you talk, pay attention to what you are actually saying and thinking.
2. Look for words/phrases like: always, never, I just am ..., I am ..., etc.
3. Look for feelings that are very strong about something.
4. At this point, just notice what you say, think, and feel.
5. Say: "Oops. There's a rule." And let it go.
6. Take a moment and decide what rule you would actually like to have. You can rewrite your rules to benefit you. (Remember to let go of the word "not.")

REM:

Repetition: The more often you do this, the easier it will become.

Emotion: Feel excited about the discovery of your rules. This excitement will bring more rules to your conscious mind and thus allow you to know what you are actually thinking, saying, and feeling.

Motion: This exercise can be done at any time, while you are doing anything.

Purpose:

These are words that limit you in some way. By their very nature, they block off other possibilities. However, by opening yourself to the idea that there are other possibilities out there, you will be able to recognize what your rules are, how to change them, and how to be happier, more at peace, and living in the love feeling.

Prayer

Help From the Universe

Prayers are the last way (although some people may say they are the first) for letting the Universe (and yourself) know where you desire to go or what you hope to happen or have. They involve faith and acknowledgment of something outside yourself. With a prayer, we accept that we can't directly see "who" we are asking for help from, but we have the faith that whoever that someone is, He will help us. Prayer acknowledges that there is a higher source. Remember: just because we can't see something using the methods we currently have for measurement, doesn't mean that something isn't there. We just can't see it ... yet.

Over the years, people have been conditioned to recite the religious prayers as they are written. Now, I'm not saying that they are wrong; however, if you don't have a lot of feeling behind them, then all you are doing is reciting words, making the prayer weaker.

I'm a big believer in prayers and God. I even have a sign in my bathroom where I put on my makeup to remind me of God's answers ... Yes. Not yet. I have something better in mind. (Ha! Do you see the joke about makeup and something better in mind?)

I know this isn't about prayers directly, but my path to believing in a Higher Power, which is the first step to prayer, was in believing in something bigger than myself. After all, faith, believing, and trust are all interrelated and necessary. I had a few experiences in my life that helped me believe that there is something more "out there." Now, I'm comfortable with the idea and have a simple rule to support this ... *A Higher Power is ready, willing, and able to help me at all times ... however, the answer may be better than I expect.* (Do you see how the sign in my bathroom played into helping me make this rule? Or was it that I already believed it and agreed with the sign, and that's why I got the sign to begin with?)

In 2003, Dr. Ron Jahner (my naturopathic physician, energy expert, and later my mentor) said that he'd taken me as far as he could at that time in regard to my headaches. He'd heard about a woman in California who had great results as a medical intuitive. I'm interested in the weird and strange; and knowing that there was a cure for headaches out there somewhere, I said, "Let's go."

So we flew to California. As I laid on her massage table face-down, Dr. Jahner sat at the head of the table, and Anamika (the medical intuitive ... very good, look her up) sat by my right side. She said, "To get rid of your headaches, you need to get rid of your husband." My right hip went "clunk" as if it had been held up and was just dropped. I resisted this advice for about eight months, but the Universe gave me plenty of signs until my then-husband and I decided to go our separate ways.

Up to that point, I'd never considered ending my marriage, so I tried to save it. But Anamika had planted the seed, and I started to take a look at what our marriage really was. The more I brought up that we needed to change things, the more evident it was that my then-husband didn't care to do so. After eight months, we decided that what we had wasn't working for either of us. It was right then that we got to decide what our relationship would be like from that point forward. We actually hugged and cried as we decided to separate, knowing that we were making a difficult but right decision for us.

This experience with Anamika (and her open-mindedness) intrigued me, and I searched for more information, which led me to another teacher, Belinda Womack (an angel communicator). I was a little wary, but I was open to learning about this mysterious Higher Power. And I'm very glad that I did. The feeling that I don't have to do it all on my own—that I'm a part of something bigger and that help is available for the asking—is very comforting.

Prayer Guidelines

Through the years, various people have helped me "communicate" with this Higher Power. Here are a few guidelines for prayers that I've collected.

1. Always be respectful and polite. After all, no one wants to help you when you are being mean. (Do you notice the rule? *Being polite and respectful brings help.* Or *being polite and respectful makes life smoother.*)

2. Ask for what you desire instead of what you don't want. Use positive language and forget about the word "not." People think in pictures, and there is no picture for "not." And for some reason, the Universe doesn't hear the word "not." So if you are asking, "God, please give me a kid who doesn't talk back." The Universe will bring you someone who *does* talk back. It is better to ask, "Please allow for my child to be polite and respectful to me and others."

3. Ask with feeling. The more feeling you have, the stronger the prayer is, since the Universe knows what you truly desire because of the feeling attached to it.

4. Step aside. Once you have asked for the help, step aside
   and let the Universe bring it to you. If you are holding
   on to a specific outcome, the Universe may think you
   haven't let go yet, and it won't start working on your
   prayer.

When I first started praying, I didn't even know what to say.
Belinda gave me a formula. "Mother, Father, God, I am willing
to experience the miracle of ..." She directed the prayer to the
Divine Mother, Divine Father, and God. This covered the femi-
nine and masculine aspects of God. (She also taught about the
specific archangels and would ask directly for help from them.)

This prayer formula opened the doorway to allow something different. The way it is worded ... "willing to experience
the miracle of" ... automatically turns your attention to what it
is you DO desire.

Belinda encouraged us (the class) to write down the prayers.
By doing this, we are more thoughtful about what we write, and
the prayers are easier to let go. We don't have to hold onto it in
our minds.

By writing down my prayers, an interesting thing happened.
When I went back years later and reviewed the prayers, I found
that they were all fulfilled in some way. They may not have
shown up as I expected—and many times the outcome was
even better—but I had the result of the prayer ... and I didn't
need to constantly focus on it. I did, however, follow the subtle
signs that popped up in my life and in this way "worked" toward
my intentions.

Prayers can be said (and not written down). This is especially helpful if the goal is immediate; for example, with traffic.
However, be aware that the intentions, rules, and expectations
will play a role in how this is fulfilled.

Let's take the example of finding a parking space. If you have the rule *parking spaces are always where I need them*, then they will be because you expect them to be. Or you can say a prayer, trust that a higher source will fulfill it for you, and then park accordingly. But again, you have to trust (expect, have faith) that it will be fulfilled.

Seeing the Perfection – Where's the Good?

An easy way to accept what does happen is to have a rule that *whatever happens is perfect*. This doesn't mean that everything goes your way; but instead, it allows you to find the perfection in what does happen.

Let's take the parking space scenario again. You say a prayer, set the expectation, have a rule, or however you go about it, but the parking space isn't exactly where you expected. Where is the good? Where is the perfection? You might know what it is ... you'd been moaning and groaning about not getting enough exercise, and this parking space is further away, thus giving you a chance to walk (a form of exercise). Or you might not know what the good is ... the Universe knows that something bad may happen if you had the parking space you thought you should have and is saving you from experiencing it. Again, trust that *what shows up is for your benefit*.

By allowing yourself to trust, life becomes easier because you aren't constantly fighting or being disappointed in what does show up. You are constantly looking for the good, which ultimately makes you feel better, and then this good feeling attracts better to you.

CHAPTER 7
Consciousness Concept Review

Prayer/Prayer Guidelines/Seeing the Perfection

▶ Just because we can't see something using the methods we currently have for measurement doesn't mean that something isn't there. We just can't see it ... yet.

▶ When praying:

> Be respectful and polite

> Ask for what you do desire.

> Ask with feeling.

> Let go of how you think the specific outcome will be.

▶ Prayer opens the doorway to allow something different.

▶ Look for the perfection in what does happen.

Prayer Exercise

How to do it:

1. Say or write: "Mother, Father, God, I'm willing to experience the miracle of…" (Or use another formula that works for you.)
2. Complete the sentence with what you desire.
3. Let it go.
4. When an action comes up to support your prayer, do it.

REM:

Repetition: A single prayer can have a big influence. But the more prayers you write down (or say), the easier it becomes, the more you trust that the prayer will be answered, and the more answers show up.

Emotion: The stronger your desire, the stronger your prayer … as long as your true feelings match up with what you are asking for in the prayer.

Motion: Writing a prayer is the motion. The act of writing involves more senses and thus more of you is involved in the prayer.

Purpose:

Prayers open the possibility that a higher source will help you achieve your desires.

Choice

We Each Have a Choice in How We React

When we make decisions, we are in fact making choices. Things happen all around us, and it's our choice how we react and respond to whatever is happening.

Whatever you are feeling very often dictates what the reaction is in that moment. Ideally, you will get to such a neutral space that the best action can step forward, and this action isn't controlled by your feelings in the moment. You can make the choice to be neutral.

Think about this for a minute. When your teen is yelling and screaming about something, does it help that you also yell and scream? Probably not. When your teenager is upset, do you have to be upset? No. You can choose to feel and behave another way.

In every moment, you have a choice. What is your choice right now? Once you realize that it's a choice, you can choose how you want it to be. You can choose how much you want to be the same or different. You can choose if you want the change to be instantaneous or happen over time. (*Is it okay to shift gradually so your mind and body are more comfortable with the change? Or do you want the entire shift now?*)

You can choose to play the game of life in any way you choose to play it. Be aware of that choice. You aren't a victim—you are only trying on experiences. Keep the ones that work for you and stop focusing on the ones that don't. But through it all, remember that you are not the experiences. They are just experiences. The real you (spirit, higher self, etc.) is watching the game of life you choose to play.

It's your choice what you do, but each choice has a natural consequence. Take time to evaluate which consequence will help you reach your intentions. The more all of these work together, the easier it will be.

Coherence is Working Together

When things are in coherence (all working together), your spirit, mind, emotions, and body are all feeling great. Equate this to your family communicating very well. Everyone listens when someone is talking, and they take turns responding. Throughout the entire conversation, people are respectful and kind. It's easy and feels open, expansive, and light. (Remember the truth barometer?)

However, when things are not in coherence (not working together), it feels like sandpaper. Everyone's nerves are on edge as you try to have a constructive conversation. No one listens. Everyone talks over everyone else, all while getting louder and louder in an effort to be heard. This feeling is more constrictive, closed-in, and heavy.

Very often how we react is just a habit. It's how we've always done it. It's how our parents reacted. It's how *their* parents reacted. But you can make a different choice. Just because you've done it that way in the past doesn't mean your reaction has to be that way in the present or future.

Feelings are signals that something in the body and your experiences is or isn't in coherence. Imagine 100 cars on a highway driving north at 60 mph. They are all going in the same direction, at the same speed, and are coherent. Their combined energy is very strong.

Now imagine if one of these cars turned around and drove against traffic. The cars are no longer coherent. Horns would blare, and cars would swerve to get out of the way. The horns are equivalent to the feeling of pain, constriction, or heaviness. They are letting you know that something isn't right and things aren't all hunky-dory. There is a contradiction.

When one car goes the wrong direction, it's equivalent to stubbing your toe. But when fifty cars go the wrong way, that is equivalent to something much more painful, such as peripheral neuropathy (a disease that causes the nerves in the hands and feet to feel like they are on fire constantly).

In an ideal world, we are all working toward coherence, which feels better. And the better we feel, the closer we come to uncovering the joy that is already within us.

Using Coherence in Your Life

So what does this mean for you? You have a choice. Do you want to be coherent in your body and your life? Do you want to be coherent with your family? Are you willing to look at everything and listen to the messages when you are not coherent? In the end, it's your life and your choice.

Let's make the assumption that you would like to feel lighter and more coherent. (After all, if you wanted to feel worse, you wouldn't be reading this book.) To begin with, make the conscious choice to notice what you feel.

For a simple example, think of something—anything. If you feel open, expansive, and light, it is good for you and can be your truth. One of my friends says she sees the truth choice literally light up. That's her way of doing it.

Or do you feel constrictive, closed in, and heavy? Do you feel as if you've been kicked in the gut on a feeling level? In this case, whatever you are thinking of isn't right for you. It's not in your best interest, and it's not your truth. And it doesn't even matter what everyone else says. You know the truth for you.

This works when you are deciding anything, even what to eat. Try it the next time you are at a restaurant. Choose two things on the menu. How does the thought of them make you feel? Pay attention. At first, the feelings may be feather soft. But as with anything, the more you practice it, the better you get. After a while, you will notice that you can automatically choose those things that make you feel light and expansive. It can show up as a feeling, a knowing, or a sense. But however it shows up is right.

This truth doesn't even have to match up with what other people think is best for you. Compare it to your teen making choices for college … which school, major, living situation, location, activities, etc. You may think you know what is best; but if he pays attention to his own feelings, he will know what is best. And if he makes his choices based on what feels expansive and light, he will be happier and more joyful.

And I'm making the assumption that as a great parent, you want your child to be self-sufficient and confident with his own decisions. And just like you would like to feel and follow your truths, I'm sure you would like to teach your child how to do the same.

CHAPTER 8
Consciousness Concept Review
. . . .
Choice/Coherence

▶ You can choose to play the game of life in any way you choose to play it.

▶ You aren't a victim. All you are doing is trying on experiences.

▶ Coherence is when your spirit, mind, emotions, and body are all working together.

▶ How we react is usually a habit.

▶ You know the truth for you.

▶ Feelings pop up to tell you something is or isn't working for you.

▶ When things aren't coherent, you are out of balance.

. . . .

Increasing Your Vibration Exercise

How to do it:

1. Choose an activity that is a higher vibration than where you are and makes you feel better and lighter.
   a. Spiritual reading
   b. Prayers
   c. Being in nature
   d. Saying, "I'm grateful for …."
   e. Finding the good in things
   f. Doing something nice for someone else
   g. Writing about all the great stuff happening in your life
   h. Sharing love with something or someone else …
      in short, feeling the love
2. Do it.

REM:

Repetition: Whenever you want to increase your vibration, you can do a new activity (of course the more you do, the better you feel).

Emotion: The better you feel, the more you want to feel better, so the more you do to feel better.

Motion: It depends on the activity as to how much motion it requires. The more you move your body and the more senses you include, the stronger the outcome will be.

Purpose:

You are making a choice to feel better and attract more good into your life.

Hint:

Whatever you do first thing in the day sets the tone/vibration for the day.

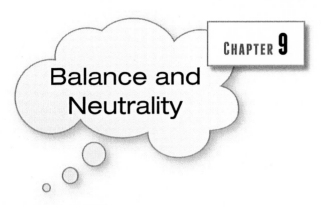

Balance and Neutrality

Neutralizing ... Getting to the Calm Feeling

We've done the first step: paying attention to your feelings. Now that you can feel the feelings, let's neutralize them. What? First we feel the feelings and then we get rid of them? But won't we need them to know what is right?

Feelings pop up to tell you something is or isn't working for you. These feelings are only there to help you. They let you know when things are not coherent ... when you are out of balance. The more you balance your feelings, the more neutral they become, and they no longer pull you in a direction that doesn't work for you. Remember ... the more coherent you feel, the easier the game of life becomes.

Neutralizing is about getting to the calm place within you so that you don't have a knee-jerk reaction. Our feelings have energy attached to them. It's usually this energy that charges the experience and directs us to take specific actions, which lead to certain results. If we can neutralize the charge and change the energy, then the actions we choose will most likely be different, and thus the result will be different.

Try looking at it like this: you are standing erect. This is the unconditioned you—your truth, who you are before you have collected all the beliefs that have conditioned you. Now put on a backpack, the first belief that will condition you. You are still able to stand erect. Add a rock, another belief. There is a subtle shift in your posture, but you are still erect. As you add more and more rocks (beliefs), your posture shifts.

The erect you is now buried under all of the beliefs you have collected. And to add another element, each rock is covered in mud. This mud equals all the feelings you cling to about the belief. And guess what? The mud dries and becomes dirt that doesn't stay just on the rocks. Your body and all the beliefs are then covered in the dirt.

If you were asked to stand erect (know your truth), you might be able to for a moment; but overall, you wouldn't be able to stay erect until you shed the rocks (the beliefs) and dirt (all the feelings you have collected about the beliefs).

To begin, start from where you are. Feel the feelings you have. Then remove the rocks one by one to "wash" away the dirt (feelings) until you feel neutral so that you can return to the erect person you are underneath—your truth—the person you were born to be. And guess what? This erect you is a happy you! This person is the joyful you that you already are, just no longer covered up in rocks and dirt.

Feelings are Balanced

Neutrality is the point where your feelings are balanced. It is the point where you are okay if the event happens or if it doesn't happen. Once you achieve neutrality, you will be able to make a decision about the next right action to take *without* your feelings interfering. The next right actions will become more obvious and very often just fall into your lap.

Here's an example of how quickly things can move when you get your feelings in line with your desires. Adam, my youngest, had braces on his teeth. They were taking their sweet time to move since he didn't like to wear the rubber bands. In our old way of thinking, we thought that the rubber bands determined how fast the teeth moved. However, one day on the way to the orthodontist, Adam asked me to shift the energy. He wanted to get the braces off. I laughed about it, but gave it a try. Using hand balancing,[4] we brought up all his feelings about having and not having the braces. We brought up all of my feelings about both. Then we dropped into our hearts found the feeling of love and settled into this feeling. I was neutral on the subject. If it happened, great! If it didn't, oh well. Adam totally visualized that the braces would be off and that his smile would be great. Boy was I surprised when the orthodontist said that the next appointment would be to take the braces off!

In this example, the timing was immediate. Things can happen that fast. It's only our belief that it takes a long time that prevented it from showing up earlier. This is the opposite of what many people believe. *Braces take time.* That is the general belief. Everyone agrees on this rule. And because everyone agrees, the morphic field (the strength of the belief) is very strong. The stronger the morphic field is, the less likely that something else can show up ... but it is possible. To have something else show up, you must line up your personal beliefs with the feelings you truly desire.

One thing that I've noticed is that as I've become more neutral—my intuition has sharpened. Taking the charge off the feelings of the situation has let me really "see" what is happening.

---

[4] The hand balancing exercise can be found at the end of this chapter.

Balance the Energy in Your Hands

It's time to learn how to be neutral. There are lots of methods out there that teach you this. They are all good, but the one that I use the most is one Dr. Ron Jahner, my mentor, taught me. It's called hand balancing.

With hand balancing you are measuring the energy of two ideas and feeling which has more energy attached to it. From there, you are balancing the energy of the two ideas until they weigh the same, which is a way to know that you aren't holding onto one more than the other. They are neutral. The net result of this is that you feel better, opening the doorway for even better things to come into your life.

How long does this take? It can take as long as you want. If you have 30 seconds at a stoplight, you can do a quick one or two. If you have half an hour, you can do more balancing and neutralizing.

You can also do it with a friend. This helps me stick with it longer. You see, I get distracted and forget I'm doing the exercises if I just sit and stare into space as I do hand balancing. For me, I do better if I add an action such as writing, typing, dancing, or twirling in circles. Yes, twirling in circles. Dr. Jahner always knows when the topic is harder for me because I can't sit, and I start doing full turns as we balance the energy. I even imagine the energy as if it's a tornado spinning away from me.

How do you know when something is neutral and balanced? Your hands will feel like they weigh the same. Or you will have another physical sign such as a big sigh or yawn to let you know that the energy shifted.

When I first started doing this, I was so detached that I couldn't feel my feelings, so this was very difficult. It took me 45 minutes to balance the energy of *one* pair of thoughts! Now,

I'm much more connected with my feelings, and I can usually neutralize within five seconds.

A really cool thing is that it doesn't matter what your thoughts are to get started. Just the process of balancing and neutralizing will affect everything in your life. It's just getting the ball rolling. You can balance "red" and "blue." Or you can do opposites such as "peace" and "hate." Or you can take situations such as "finishing writing this book easily and effortlessly" and "never in a million years finishing this book."

Notice that with the last one, I added the extremes. The more extreme the two thoughts are, the more feelings you have, thus more pop up to be neutralized.

The thoughts can even be funny. Imagine in one hand I have the thought of finishing writing this book, but I've added a picture of me dancing with the finished manuscript. Maybe it's a waltz. Stars zing out of my finished manuscript as I hug it and dance. In the other hand, I have a picture of me chained to my desk and typing as the sun circles the earth over and over. My hair grows longer and longer, and I smell from never stopping long enough to shower. Plates of leftover food are piled up on my desk. Each picture has a feeling. It is the feeling that we are balancing.

An unusual thing to note is that very often, the opposite of what you think to be the problem will have the heaviest energy. In the above example, it would be logical to assume that the never finishing picture would be heavier. But in reality, I've started many manuscripts before and haven't finished them, so this feels normal to me. It's the actual finishing that has a heavier energy. In other words, I have more feelings associated with finishing the manuscript because it is a new experience, and I don't know what it will feel like. It is a fear of the unknown. I don't know how my life will change if I finish writing this book.

Balancing the Homework Issue

The following are a few of the balancing thoughts that may pop up around the idea of a common teen-parent issue: homework. It will be from the parent's point of view. (Although the same thoughts could be from the teenager's viewpoint.) In this example, I'm assuming the parent is trying to balance and neutralize his own feelings about the teenager's experiences with not doing the homework. By the parent balancing and neutralizing his own feelings, his reaction to the teenager's actions will be different and thus allow something different to show up.

Notice that as one pair of ideas is balanced, another will appear and be ready for their turn. (I've highlighted the thought that had more energy when I did the exercise. It doesn't have to be logical. Pay attention to what *your* subconscious mind brings up and trust it.)

Do homework – Never do homework

Pleasing myself – Pleasing other people

My teen will fail if he doesn't do homework and will never succeed in life – He will learn a lesson and choose to do his homework

Homework has to be done on my time schedule – Homework can be done when he "feels like it"

His schedule – My schedule

Teaching responsibility and follow through by completing homework – Teaching natural consequences from not doing homework

I have to maintain control – My teen is smart and can figure it out

I can let my teen take responsibility for the quality of the work – I have to oversee the homework to make sure it's done right and there aren't any mistakes

Being a helicopter parent– Stepping away

Know what the bleep I'm doing – Relying on other people

Confidence – Uncertainty

Believe in myself – Never believing in myself

Believe in myself – Oranges

Sweet – Sour (Reminds me of Chinese food.)

Teen choosing to do more homework – My telling the teen to stop

Will this change my teen's behavior? Maybe ... Maybe not. But it will change my feelings about the whole thing. I'll be calmer and not as bothered by his choices. As a result, he may choose something different. After all, how I behave is my choice, and how he behaves is his choice. Of course, as a parent, you will have a dialogue with your teen—probably many. As you do this, try to keep your reactions in check (it's best if you can be neutral). The more neutral you are, the less reactionary you will be.

If you can look at everything as perfect ... in some way ... then you open yourself to finding what is good about what is happening. Perhaps allowing the teen to fail a test freshman year, and thus recognizing for himself that his studying for the test is directly related to his success, will motivate him to succeed for himself. This is a vastly different internal dialogue than "I'm doing it because my mom or dad is pushing me to." The pushing scenario may eventually lead to making the choice not to study later in his school career, possibly when it is more important to not fail.

I find that it's an ongoing process that never seems to end; but then as life gets better and better, I want to see how much better it can be. It's a game, and neutralizing energy gets easier and easier, so the game is more fun to play. *Life is a game.* As *things get easier, they get better.* Or is it *as things get better, they get easier.* (Do you see the rules that pop up?)

And who cares if any of the ideas are "true." It brought up emotions to balance and neutralize. This by itself is good because the more feelings I neutralize, the more my happy, unconditioned self can come through. Remember to look for the feeling. Feel it. Balance and neutralize the feeling, then let it go. Why carry around a whole lot of baggage that you don't need to even lift?

The key is to balance everything … great, good, bad, and horrible. However, at some point, concentrate on balancing the good and the great. It took me over a year of hearing this until I really got it. (*I must be a slow learner.* Oops. There's a rule that can be dropped.) But the point is this: what you focus on is what you get—so focus on the good, and the better, and the even better than that.

CHAPTER 9
Consciousness Concept Review
. . . .
Balance and Neutrality

▶ Neutralizing is about getting to the calm place within you so that you don't have a knee-jerk reaction.

▶ Start from where you are.

▶ When your emotions are balanced or neutral, you are emotionally okay if the event happens OR if it doesn't happen.

▶ As you become more neutral, your intuition sharpens and the more your happy, unconditioned self can come through.

▶ Focus on balancing the good and the great (as well as the not-so-good and the not-so-great).

. . . .

Hand Balancing Exercise

How to do it:

1. Take a deep breath, exhale, then breath normally.
2. Hold your hands, palms up, with your elbows at your waist as if you are holding a tray.
3. Put a thought in one hand.
4. Put a different thought in the other hand.
5. Feel which is heavier. Yes, one will actually feel heavier.
6. Pour the energy from one hand into the other. Then reverse.
7. Repeat over and over.
8. Notice when both hands feel like they are the same and the thoughts "weigh" the same. You are now neutral and balanced.
9. Pay attention to the thoughts that pop up and use these thoughts to guide you with the next ideas to balance.

REM:

Repetition: Once is great, but more is better. The more you do this, the faster and easier it will be, the more neutral you will feel, and the sharper your intuition will be.

Emotion: Settling into your heart helps you feel what is there. The more you feel the feelings, the easier it is to neutralize them.

Motion: The movement of the hands with an idea or thought in them helps keep you focused. Eventually, you'll be able to hold your hands and feel the emotions without knowing exactly what you are balancing without a label.

Purpose:

This exercise is a way to balance or neutralize emotions/feelings. The more neutral you are, the less of a knee-jerk reaction you have and the better your intuition becomes.

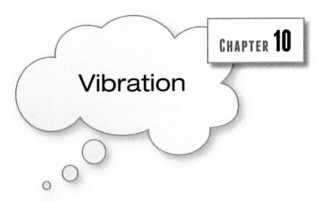

Vibration

Energy is Measured in Vibrations

Energy is the force that allows everything to happen. It is measured in vibrations and felt through feelings. The Universe works through vibration, and everything vibrates ... people, animals, plants, food, clothing, colors, pictures, words, thoughts, feelings ... everything! The vibration sends out a signal to everything else in the Universe. This signal (vibration) looks for other signals that are the same to "hang out with" and attracts those things to the original signal. This is called attraction.

Think of a high school. The students form groups based upon similar feelings, outlooks, habits, and interests, which are really just thoughts and feelings. We think of these as cliques. The students want to be with others who are "the same" as them. They attract fellow students who are "the same" or have the same vibe.

Feelings that vibrate together stay together. We tend to get in a rut with our feelings and feel the same ones over and over. It's almost like we have a set point and don't venture too far from it. However, *it doesn't have to be this way.* We can choose to have a different feeling. We can choose to walk up (or down) the feeling scale.

A feeling scale? Feelings are grouped together. Think of a piano. The low notes have similar feelings, while the higher notes feel different. A feeling scale works much the same way. Every feeling has a vibration.

On one end are the so-called "sad, depressed" feelings, while on the other end are the "joyous, peaceful" feelings. In between are a whole lot of other feelings. As you "walk" up the scale, you feel better and better because you are getting closer to the happy feelings.[5]

Something strange happens along the way—life gets easier! When you are feeling depressed, life is hard and you don't have a lot of energy to get things done. As you feel better, you have more energy and everything gets easier.

Remember the Universe restaurant? The order is based on whatever you feel strongest about. So, how do you change your order? By changing your feeling, which is a vibration. All you have to do is find what feels good for you. Then find what feels better and then what feels even better than that. The better you feel, the higher your vibration goes, and the easier it is to manifest what you actually desire in your life.

Vibrations either attract or repel. If the vibrations are alike, then they attract. And if they are different, they repel. How this works is simple. You reach for a better thought . . . a better feeling.

Can It Get Better?

Allowing for better is raising the vibration, which may lead to a better outcome. It's simple. All you have to do is ask the question. Can it be even better than that?[6] You don't have to answer or figure out how it will happen. Just ask.

---

[5] For a very good explanation, read *Power vs. Force*, by Dr. David Hawkins.
[6] All the programs have this idea. This exact question is from Access Consciousness.

Adam was upset because a friend of his was going to drink alcohol, and he thought she would make stupid mistakes because of this. So, I asked him a few questions and ended with, "And can it get better than that? And even better than that? And even better than that?" We let it go and went out of town as planned.

As it turns out, it did get better. While she did start to drink, it didn't last long. One girlfriend threw up on Adam's friend's boots. She texted Adam about what happened. Adam and I laughed, and I asked if it could get better than that! She texted again: her other girlfriend threw up on her also. She ended up not drinking a lot and just took care of her friends.

It certainly didn't show up how we expected. But it was better, and she didn't make stupid mistakes because of the drinking. (Although if I were to pass judgment, I might think underage drinking is stupid, but I'm not into judging. She is having an experience. But in this case, oh what a good one. Oops, there's judging again.)

I Love You. I Love You. I Love You.

When I was first learning about vibrations attracting and repelling, Dr. Jahner had me saying "I love you" over and over. We were raising my vibration . . . as love is a very high vibration. Then just as we finished, Shoshanna (my daughter) called from college. She was screaming and yelling about something. It doesn't matter what, because this was her norm. With Dr. Jahner's encouragement, I kept saying "I love you" over and over silently in my head. I didn't speak; I only thought it and felt it in my heart. In a relatively short period of time, Shoshanna said, "Oh forget it. I'll figure it out myself." Then she hung up. We laughed as before this, I would have gotten swept up in her drama and tried to help her, which would only prolong her complaining.

So what happened? To begin with, while Dr. Jahner and I were practicing raising my vibration, Shoshanna, who is connected to me energetically, couldn't find me in the energetic cosmos. I'd changed. She felt lost because something was different, so she reached out to me as best she could by calling and yelling. However, I wouldn't play the game. I had made a decision to have a higher vibration by repeating "I love you." She then had a choice. Did she want to rise to my vibration, or did she want to leave the vibration that felt uncomfortable? She chose to leave. (Don't worry … she didn't leave forever. She eventually decided to move up the vibrational scale and feel better.)

Being Willing To Do Something Different

Another way to look at it is that vibrations are a frequency that is given off. And just like with a radio station, you look for the frequency that is clear, agrees with you, and makes you feel "right"—something that you can identify with at that moment. Over time, you tend to stick to the same radio stations because they feel right. They feel "right" because you are familiar with them, not because one is more "right" than another.

To change your vibration to something better, you first have to be willing to change. You have to do something different. After all, if you do what you've always done, you'll get what you've always gotten. *To get something different, you have to do something different.* This is just like when I did something different (saying "I love you" in my head), and I got something different (Shoshanna didn't pull me into her drama, and she figured it out on her own).

So what is an example for your own life? Have you ever gone to a gathering feeling great but got stuck in the corner listening to negative people complain about everything? What happened? You either chose to leave (because you couldn't stand the negative talk, which was a lower energy than yours), or you stayed and started feeling negative (because you lowered your vibration to their level). When your vibrations are negative, that's what you attract; but you do not have to keep vibrating at that level. It is possible to maintain your higher vibration, but then the negative people would find excuses to leave you. One of these could happen. But what really happens is the vibrations realign and find like vibrations.

I don't know about you, but when I read a book and the main character behaves in a low-vibrational way (whining, helpless, depressed, etc.), then I tend to unconsciously adopt those feelings. The same is true if the character feels very good about him/herself. The higher the vibration of the character, the better I feel.

If you want to be successful, do you think it will be easier to be successful if you associate with people who are already successful? Or with people who are going nowhere in life and sitting on their butts watching TV and drinking every night? And if you are one of those people who is watching TV and drinking every night, you have a decision to make: Stay where you are or do something different.

Does this apply only to people? No. Vibrations apply to everything—the books you read, the movies you see, the colors you wear, the things you surround yourself with—everything! Go to a time when you were in your closet trying on clothes. For whatever reason, some outfits didn't "feel" right even though they fit. Their vibration didn't match yours at that time. If you want to be successful, then dress successful. If you want to be slovenly, then you better not dress sharp. Move your vibration in the direction you choose.

You are the one choosing, so all of this indicates that you are taking responsibility for your life. Yes, you. It all has to do with your personal vibration. Because we attract what we think and feel, we attract things, experiences, items, etc. into our lives. No one else is doing it—you are! Everyone else is attracting what they are vibrating. To each of us, what we attract is our "reality." Here's a clue ... we can change our reality.

So you may as well focus on what it is you desire, because what you focus on is what your energy is moving toward.

What You Surround Yourself With is What You Become

The words we choose also have vibrations, and these vibrations have an effect on everyone. For example, swear words and sarcasm have a different effect than loving words. The words you use matter. The words you absorb matter. The words you think matter. What you surround yourself with is what you become. Just like when we were talking about absorbing the vibrations of those we hang out with, we absorb the vibrations of the words around us.

What we put into our bodies does affect us whether it is a book, a movie, or food. When we feed the mind with high-vibrational literature, we feel better than when we read something trashy. I know this is a hard concept to accept if you love romance novels as I do. However, when I read them, I'm wallowing in the wanting of the characters and all their drama, which is basically everything going wrong in their lives. And guess what? I feel their feelings and actually feel depressed. So, over time, I've replaced the novels with more spiritual literature and feel better more of the time ... although every once in a while I'll fall off the wagon and read a romance or mystery. But as I start to feel down, I realize that I've just given my mind junk food, and it is time for something nutritious—something with a higher vibration.

The same can be said about food. I'm sure you have noticed that if you eat a diet of donuts, chocolate, and soda, you feel crummy. The more you eat healthy food, the better you feel and the clearer your mind can function.

A quick story about food: JT, my son, went on a NOLS trip; camping, sailing, hiking, and kayaking in Mexico for three months. He even got college credit. Anyway, he ate very healthy food and no sugar. When he came home, he splurged on a giant pixie stick and just about jumped out of his skin. This was a great lesson. When he eats healthy, he feels good, and when he eats junk food, he feels horrible.

So, take a look at the diet of food, language, and vibration you are feeding yourself. If you don't feel good, look for the higher vibration—something healthier. *The highest vibration wins.*

Reaching for the right words to say and write is a skill that can be developed ... if you don't already have it. Just think of what the feeling is you are trying to convey. Then find a word that matches that feeling.

As you are looking for the words that are right, be aware that the mind thinks in pictures and cannot see the word "not." Try to think of two elephants not fighting. The image that comes to mind first is two elephants fighting. How we use language is much the same. We create what we think, feel, talk about, etc. So, the words that we use will serve us better if we use open language. Closed language doesn't allow for options. Open language allows for multiple possibilities.

▶ Closed language: "I don't want a headache."

▶ Open language: "I allow the possibility that I can feel great."

In the first example, a headache is brought to the forefront of my mind, so that is what I will feel. If I rephrase it, I allow the possibility that I can feel great, which can show up in many ways, not just being pain free.

CHAPTER 10
Consciousness Concept Review

Vibration/Can It Get Better?

▶ Energy is the force that allows everything to happen. It is measured in vibrations and felt through feelings.

▶ When you have a low vibration (such as when you feel depressed), life is hard and you don't have a lot of energy.

▶ When you have a high vibration (such as when you feel happy), life is easier, and you have more energy to live the day.

▶ The higher your energy vibration, the more energy you have and the easier your life is.

▶ If you do what you've always done, you'll get what you've always gotten.

▶ You absorb vibrations from everything around you ... the people you talk to, the books you read, the music you listen to, the TV you watch, the food you eat, etc.

▶ You send vibrations out through your feelings, the words you use, the intentions you set for yourself, etc.

▶ If you don't feel good, look for a higher vibration.

▶ Highest coherent vibration wins.

YES! Exercise

How to do it:

1. Whenever you have a thought, say the word, "YES!"

REM:

Repetition: The more you do it, the better you feel.

Emotion: Say "YES" with emphasis and enthusiasm.

Motion: No motion is needed. However, a movement (such as fist pump) gives it more emphasis and moves the energy more.

Purpose:

"YES" is a very high-vibration word. Just saying it increases your vibration and allows you to feel better.

(This is a very good exercise to do when you wake up in the middle of the night and your mind is filled with random worries. Say "YES" and acknowledge to yourself that you are thinking whatever you are thinking. Saying YES over and over will shift your energy and allow you to either go back to sleep or get up and do an inspired action.)

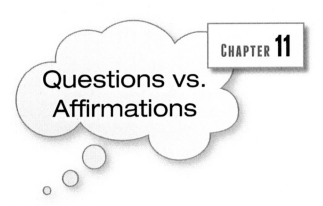

Questions vs. Affirmations

Questions Allow for Possibilities

Many people use affirmations or statements that tell the Universe who they are. For example, "I am feeling great." The idea is to raise their vibration to a better feeling. However, affirmations don't seem to work with me because while one side of my brain is saying the positive statement, the other side of my brain is negating it. It is hard to believe "I am feeling great" if my subconscious mind is pulling up all the reasons that I'm not.

Affirmations don't always work because they can set up polarity, opposites, or judgments. In the above example, "I feel great" causes the polar opposite to pop up in my head. Polarity doesn't allow movement, and it only gives two choices.

To get the same message across, try asking yourself a question instead of making a statement. This allows for wiggle room and doesn't limit the choices, as the possibilities are infinite. This shifts the energy, you will feel better, and you will have more clearly defined what you desire. This will allow all the possibilities, not just the ones you can think of in that moment. After all, if you knew what to do, you wouldn't need more possibilities.

Asking a question is allowing the possibilities. (Whereas a statement is telling the brain and giving it a chance to argue.)

By allowing possibilities, you aren't saying it has to be a certain way, only that you can open the door to the possibility. You don't even have to open the door a lot. Cracking it open is still allowing the possibility.

> Even though _____, could I feel great anyway?
> (Think of how Tony the Tiger says "great". He puts a lot of emphasis in it, so it has a stronger feeling.)
> If it was possible, could I allow that _____?
> I wonder how many ways _____? (Okay, this one is really a statement, but with the right inflection, you can make it a question.)

Clue: If you follow the questions with an emphatic "YES!" you are giving it an even higher energy with your enthusiasm. This will help you emphasize what you really want.

It is said that things go where energy flows. This means that what you give your attention to will increase. So why not give your energy to the possibilities that you do desire. The more good thoughts you pour into your body, the more good thoughts you will have, the more good you will attract, and the better your life will be. It's all a vibrational thing.

How's That Working For You?

Asking questions buys time to allow a better possibility to show up. When my *kids do something stupid, as kids often do* (oops, there's a rule), I ask, "How's that working for you?" It gives them a chance to reevaluate without me jumping down their throats. It sure takes a lot of tension out of the situation, and we can find a better way of doing it. An added bonus is that the kid is involved in the thinking process. I'm actually teaching him to think. He isn't just reacting to my yelling, which by the way, has happened a lot less since I've started doing all this rule-shifting and neutralizing. Do I have to hold my tongue sometimes? You bet. But in the end, I'm calmer, the kid has a chance to make a better choice, and everyone is happier.

Boundaries are Necessary

I want to make it clear that while I have a lot of flexibility, I also have boundaries. However, when one of the kids oversteps the boundaries, I'm there questioning and finding a better way. But I make sure they know what the boundaries are.

Before I go onto the next step, I want to share another rule I'm teaching the kids when they make a mistake. "*I'm sorry. I made a mistake. It won't happen again.*" The "it" of course applies to whatever the mistake was, as I know there will be other mistakes.

I even use this with the kids' friends. I used it twice in one night when Adam had friends over. The first time, I came down-stairs to check on the kids and noticed that one group was in the living room and the doors to the playroom were closed. Knowing that something was up, I opened the doors. Two teens were in the beginning stages of a compromising position. I turned on the lights and said, "Put your shirts on." Then I walked out.

A minute later I called another teen, who had been avoiding me, into "my office" (the recently vacated playroom). My first question was, "How old are you?" He responded, "18." I then said, "We are dealing with "this" as adults, and it's time for you to man up. It doesn't do any good to avoid the issue." (He'd brought a flask of alcohol to my house at homecoming, but it wasn't discovered until the clean up after he'd left.) We talked and I told him, "I want you to apologize to me, say you are sorry, and then say it won't happen again. After that, you will do a chore for me (heavy lifting)." After he apologized and we decided when he would be over at my house to do the chore with Adam (who doesn't get out of trouble just because he didn't know about the alcohol), we went back to the group.

I talked with the previous two teens in front of the group and said, "The correct answer is … I'm sorry. I made a mistake." And Adam finished it with "It won't happen again." We all laughed. It's a good thing I have a great relationship with the teens. The girl was very certain that it would never happen again … at *my* house.

I didn't realize how often I say this to Adam until he finished the ending of the phrase. At least he's learning to take responsibility for his mistakes. He's also learning that mistakes happen, and life goes on. Luckily, Adam is a very level-headed kid and not too much seems to bother him. Don't get me wrong … he's had his ups and downs, but they have been flutters in the wind instead of the tidal waves his sister experienced as a teen.

When Shoshi was a teen (actually since she was born), I could never have imagined writing this book. But I have her to thank for rocking the boat and forcing me to look deeper within myself. Raising her was not a picnic. She had a lot of anger, anxiety, and depression that came bubbling out at inopportune times. It was like walking on eggshells every day. Nothing I did worked. But *I kept trying.*

When she was twelve, the school suggested that she needed more help than they could give her. They wanted her to go to a therapeutic school. I thought I could do better if I just let her sleep in (she has insomnia), so I chose to homeschool her. Big mistake. This only increased our tension.

So, we reevaluated and hired a teacher to do the homeschooling. As much as she loved him, she still couldn't pull it together.

The next step was a residential treatment center in Utah. We found a great place that was a life changer for all of us. After two stays there, she was doing much better, but I couldn't handle the possibility that her verbal abuse would return, so I sent her to a boarding school that had emotional support. She flourished and finished high school. Considering she hated school since preschool, this was a big deal.

During all of this, I stepped back from the daily turmoil, realized my marriage wasn't working, and got divorced. Now, Shoshi and I are best friends. She is progressing in her life, and when she looks back, she doesn't even know why she was so angry.

While all of this was going on, she was reacting to feelings. Then I was reacting to feelings. Then she was reacting to those feelings. You get the idea. In reality, they were just experiences that we had feelings about.

All of us react to the feelings we experience. The clue is to neutralize the energetic charge of the feelings to the point that we can see that we are in fact just having an experience.

Chapter 11
Consciousness Concept Review

Questions vs. Affirmations

- ▶ Affirmations set up polarities, opposites, or judgments.
- ▶ Questions allow possibilities and don't limit choices.
- ▶ Ask, "How's that working for you?"
- ▶ Set the appropriate boundaries (and still be neutral).

Increasing Possibilities Exercise

How to do it:

1. Look at something you don't like. (This can also be done with things you do like.)
2. Say, "I wonder how this could be different."
3. Or ask, "If it was possible, could I allow ... ?"
4. Or ask, "I wonder if it can be even better than that? And even better than that? And even better than that?"
5. Let go of expecting a certain answer from a certain place and allow the possibilities to come into your conscious mind as you go about your day.

REM:

Repetition: Doing this exercise one time may yield some new possibilities. However, the more you do this, the easier the possibilities are to recognize and the more possibilities pop up.

Emotion: Staying in a neutral space, without judging if the "answers" are right or wrong, good or bad, allows for even more possibilities to appear.

Motion: Go about your day and notice where your attention goes. Know that the answer is going to appear. You don't have to (although you can) sit and write lists and lists of possibilities. I have done it, and it helps shift the energy of the moment.

Purpose:

This exercise opens the possibilities and allows something to be different. By opening the possibilities, you are open to the vibration rising and life getting even easier.

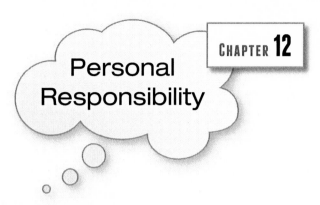

Personal Responsibility

Take Responsibility for Everything in Your Life. Change Your Reality.

You are the one choosing, so all of this indicates that you are taking responsibility for your life. Yes, you.

Everything vibrates, and we attract those experiences and things that have similar vibrations to how we are vibrating. If our thoughts and feelings vibrate—and they do—and we can change our thoughts and feelings—then it stands to reason that we can change our vibration and what we attract. If we can change it, then we have a choice as to how we desire to be. We get to make this choice, and thus we have personal responsibility.

Do your rules or beliefs start because of the things that are happening to you? Sorry to disappoint you, but no. Remember ... you have to take responsibility for everything in your life. Yes, even the stuff you don't like. But they are happening because before they happened, you had a thought and feeling that had a vibration, which matched the vibration of the experiences you attracted. The initial feeling could have happened in utero, when you were a baby, or at any other point in your life. And if you believe in spirit and the metaphysical, it could have happened in another life, a parallel universe, or some other "non-traditional" time.

Do the following experiment and see what I mean: Stand up tall, chin lifted, shoulders down and relaxed, back erect, and here is the most important part ... put a smile on your face and think about something you love. I'll see you in 20 minutes.

Welcome back. I'll bet that after 20 minutes of smiling (or five minutes if you cheated), that you are feeling better. You have done the possible—you have raised your vibration by matching your thoughts and feelings (while thinking of something you love, it's hard not to feel the love), and then taking an action (standing at attention and smiling) to support them. It is all up to you.

Life is About Your Possibility Chain

Remember the possibility chain (Stimulus-Belief-Thought-Feeling-Action-Review)? In the above example, the stimulus (my asking you to do something), led to a perception (It's easy to do), which led to a belief (I can allow that), and thought (I can stand straight and smile. I'm interested to see if that changes my feelings). Once you allowed yourself to do the exercise, you had a gut reaction. You could feel your feelings as you started and as they changed. We are looking for the change. (If you go looking for the way you used to feel, you will be able to find it. Focus on the better feeling.) Once you feel good, you can choose the next right action.

As you go through life, you continuously do this possibility chain ... even if you aren't aware of it. By stepping in and changing something along the chain, you are taking personal responsibility. And since it's your life, you may as well choose the responsibility (and resulting feelings, actions, etc.) instead of living your life as if you are a victim. You are not a victim. You can choose something different.

CHAPTER **12**

Consciousness Concept Review

. . . .

Personal Responsibility/Possibility Chain

▶ You are not a victim.

▶ You have the choice to direct your personal responsibility.

▶ Take responsibility for your life. It's your life after all.

▶ Your vibrations attract your experiences; and since you can change your vibrations, you can change your experiences.

▶ Possibility Chain: Stimulus – Belief – Thought – Feeling – Action – Review

. . . .

Responsibility Exercise

How to do it:

1. Think of something that you thought was someone else's fault.
2. Ask yourself, "If it was possible, could I allow that I played a part in why or how this happened?"
3. Ask yourself, "What was my part in this?"
4. Listen for the answer. It may come to you as a feeling, sense, knowing, thought, or in a number of other ways.
5. Accept responsibility for your part.

REM:

Repetition: The more you accept responsibility, the less you find fault with others and yourself, the easier life becomes.

Emotion: Be neutral and open to the possibilities. You're doing this to examine and improve, not to blame.

Motion: No motion is necessary.

Purpose:

The only person you can change is yourself. So look at your part in a given situation, accept responsibility, stop blaming yourself and others, and then be open to things being different. This allows you to be proactive so that you don't keep repeating the same actions you didn't like to begin with.

Feelings

The Mind is Powerful ... But the Feelings are More So

"This all sounds like mind over matter," said my father as we were talking about what I do and this book. He continued, "I agree with that."

I could see where we differed. "But it's more than that," I began. "*It's about the feelings being congruent with the thoughts you have.* When your feelings and thoughts agree, things feel true. And when your thoughts and feelings don't agree, things feel off or false."

He thought about this and then changed the subject as we were deciding which street to turn on. We never did get back to the topic, but it got me thinking: All my life, I'd learned that *it's mind over matter*. I'd bought into this.

In fact, just before I gave birth to Shoshanna (my third child), my then-husband's back went out. He waited to do anything about it ... just in case something went wrong with his back or her birth and he missed the whole thing. So literally the day after the C-section, he got a shot in his back. When my mother told me he was fine, I remember I was standing in my hospital room at the end of my bed. I literally said, "I'm so tired of being strong." It was like a whoosh of energy went out of me, and all of a sudden I could feel the pain from the C-section. It was so obvious that I knew something amazing had just happened.

The mind is powerful. But it wasn't until years later that I realized how the agreement of the mind and the feelings were really at play in this. It was my feeling that I was tired of being strong that shifted the mind's perception.

I was congruent with being strong, until I wasn't. It's the congruency that shifted. And that's what we are trying to do by being neutral—shift the congruency of our feelings and thoughts. Learning to live in the place where we are neutral allows for the feelings to come up.

Let Go of Judgment

Neutrality doesn't mean that we don't have feelings. Neutrality isn't the heart monitor's flat-line of death. *Life is meant to be lived*—to be felt. If we pay attention to our feelings, we will know where we are not congruent with our thoughts. Then we can let go of the attachment that we are holding onto about those thoughts (aka judgment). Once we allow the possibility for something to be different, then things can be different.

However if we hold onto judgment, then we are never truly neutral. We are holding onto the feelings to prove ourselves right. And in doing so, we are pulling or pushing our emotions to fall in line with our judgments. (Remember feelings are the sensations associated with the emotions.)

Letting go of judgment is easy when you are neutral because you don't care one way or the other, and the best action just appears. You don't have an attachment to being right about one side. But sometimes it helps to have a method to go to when you do find yourself judging. To let go of judgment, try one of the following:

- Ask a question: If I could accept something different, what might that be?
- Change your focus: Great! I wonder how that will benefit me?
- Look at it in a new way: Wow! That's interesting. That's an interesting choice.
- Talk to yourself: That's amazing. Look at that. There's a feeling I didn't know I had. I wonder if there's any truth in that? I wonder what it would be like if I didn't have any judgment about this? I wonder what's right about this?

It seems that the sting of the feeling is gone once we can say, "Wow. That's amazing." We can step back and see where we are holding onto the feeling and then make a choice ... keep holding onto it or allow something different (a new possibility).

Feelings are good—they are sensations of an experience. Take excitement and fear, which are names for the sensation and are thus emotions. They feel the same. The sensation is the same. However, we tend to label one as good and one as bad. If you can go into the feeling (instead of the judgment of the emotion), you will be able to pop the feeling and let it go.

Feelings tell us where our energy is flowing or stuck. They let us know when our thoughts and feelings are congruent (or not). They are clues and signs from the Universe. We need feelings to navigate the world. Unfortunately, too many people are as shut down as I was and don't feel their feelings. And many people who do feel their feelings don't know that they have the power to change them.

This was my first challenge on my road to self-discovery— feeling my feelings. I kept getting stuck at the beginning ... afraid that *if I did feel them, I'd be hurt in some way.* But thankfully, I finally broke through with the help of some patient teachers, the idea of *not giving up,* and a knowing that *there was a better way.*

The Real Reason ... Feeling Good

The best place to start is where you are. After all, that's where you are! Why pretend otherwise? In fact, this is a very good rule: *Start from where I am*. Some people have done lots of inner work to get to the bottom of what they are all about, and others are just starting on their path of self-discovery.

But when you get down to it, the only reason ... the one underneath all the other reasons ... that we do something is because we want to feel good. We don't do anything with the idea, "I'm doing this because I want to feel worse." However, sometimes we get confused and think that feeling good in this moment will give us the big picture feeling good. Well, I'm here to tell you that it's true ... if you keep following the feel good feeling. But you can only know for sure that it feels good when you are truly neutral in the moment.

Looking for a better feeling is not judgment. We aren't saying it's right or wrong, good or bad. Judgment is saying that feeling good is the right way, while feeling sad is the wrong way. There are times when feeling sad is appropriate—we just don't want to get stuck there. When you can feel the emotions, and then let them go, you aren't holding on to the judgment of that emotion and not allowing another possibility.

Focus on the Good

This is important stuff. Pay attention to the good and put your focus here. More good will come your way. The idea of this makes sense—what you focus on is what you get. Whereas if all you do is look for the bad stuff so you can balance that and make it neutral, you will notice more bad stuff, and you will probably attract more bad stuff into your life. If you are anything like me, then you don't need more of that. Do we really need to keep track of everything bad in our lives? (I'm not saying ignore it all together, just focus on what you *do* desire.)

What we are striving for is a win-win situation. If you focus on the good, you will attract more good. However, if you focus on the negative, then that is what you will attract. So, how about with your teen? Find something good and put your focus there. What we are doing is changing your feelings. The more good you see your teen doing, the more good you will notice, and the more good that will happen. As you notice this good, you will feel better. And since one way to feel better is to reach for a better feeling, noticing the good will lead you there.

Earlier, we talked about how the thoughts came, and then there were feelings about the thoughts. Based on this, we built a way to change our thoughts. But what if you could identify the feeling you want, *then* have thoughts about that feeling? Those thoughts would reinforce the feeling. They might even change the actions you choose to take … but the feeling you are looking for would be within you. And by feeling this, you are changing your vibration. From this vibration, you will attract many things into your life to support this feeling.

Ask for Your True Desire

What is it that you truly desire? How do you move from the thought to the feeling?

Let's start with an example of thinking then feeling. The thought is "I can't stand the way my teen dresses." The feeling can be shame, embarrassment, or concern that people will get the "wrong" impression.

When you see your teen in the morning, you can start a fight about the clothes and harp on all the things that are wrong. You can nitpick about everything that isn't the way you'd like it to

be. OR you can make a choice to notice the good and let go of
any judgment you may have. Find something you like. Maybe its,
"Wow. That's a great color on you." Or "That's a very sturdy fabric.
It's going to last a long time." Or "I notice how much effort you put
into applying your makeup. Can you show me how you do it?"

In this case, notice how you feel, but comment on the good.
Keep the sarcasm out of your voice. Teens will pick up on how
you say something. So, try to be as pleasant as possible. As my
mother used to say, "*You catch more flies with honey than you
do with vinegar.*"

Or you can take the opinion of the mother of a friend of mine.
She told her son that he could dress any way he liked, as long as
he had good grades. So he went all out and had a blue Mohawk,
an earring, Goth clothing, and excellent grades. At the time, he
thought he was getting away with something; but by the time he
figured out the deal, he already had the excellent grades. And
now he is a respected businessman, a Boy Scout leader, a family
man, a good friend, and helps run the family company. His mom
knew what was important and focused on that.

Only talk about the good. This alone will change your feelings, and you will feel better because the more you notice the
good, the more you'll see the good. And by the way, stop talking
to everyone (neighbors, teachers, friends, etc.) about what you
don't like, as that will only get you more of what you don't like.

This doesn't mean that you don't have feelings about how
your teen dresses. You're just not as bothered by them as before.
What's interesting is that very often your feelings are different
from what you are complaining about. In the first example, the
parent's feelings are shame, embarrassment, or concern about
what others think. It may look like they are disappointed in their
teen; but underneath, if the parent puts it all together, it could
be a concern that the teen (as an extension of the parent) will

show the world that the parent isn't good enough in some way. After all, what will people think of the parent if the teen is that different? (There are other options, but we will go with this one for the example.)

Here is where you are playing with your energy (and leaving your teen alone). The situation of not liking the teen's clothes sets off feelings within you, the parent. Ideally, you will be neutral and look at life as interesting. (Yes, it's even interesting how the teen chooses to dress.)

Try a quick hand balancing. In one hand, put the good that you noticed. In the other hand, put the feeling that's bothering you. Now balance the two. Keep going as new ideas and feelings pop up. They are signs showing where you have energy attached to a thought. This energy can be released by noticing it, doing hand balancing, just deciding to let it go, or you can examine it and ask yourself, "What feeling am I really looking for in this moment?"

In the example, what is the feeling that the parent is actually looking for? It could be acceptance, pride, acknowledgment, recognition, or a dozen other feelings. (As a side note, the teen is probably looking for these too. He's just going about it in a different way.)

Identify the feeling and then ask, "How many ways might this feeling show up in my life?" Be open to the possibility that the feeling can appear in many different areas of your life. You don't have to know ahead of time where it will come from. It may show up as winning an award, people complimenting you, friends asking your advice, or finishing a project and having the knowing feeling that you did a great job.

Having the teen dress a certain way is only one way that you can get the feeling. Start with the feeling. This is a much simpler way to get what you desire. After all, it's really the feeling that you are going after.

And here's a hint: we are all looking for what feels good. So ask yourself, "I wonder how many ways I can feel great today?" *Then expect the best. Life will get better.*

CHAPTER 13
Consciousness Concept Review

Feelings/Judgment/Focus on the Good

▶ It's about the feelings being congruent with the thoughts you have. When your feelings and thoughts agree, things feel right. And when your thoughts and feelings don't agree, things feel off or wrong.

▶ Once you allow the possibility for something to be different, then things can be different.

▶ The primary reason we do something is to feel good.

▶ What you focus on is what you get.

▶ Talk about the good in your life. Stop talking to everyone about everything that is going wrong.

▶ Start with the feeling.

▶ Let go of judgment to allow the possibilities to flow to you.

Locate Your True Feeling Exercise

How to do it:
1. Think about something you desire.
2. Ask yourself, "What feeling am I looking for in this moment?"
3. Ask yourself, "If I had a feeling underneath this desire, what might my true desire be?"
4. Keep asking until you discover what you are truly after.
5. Stay open to the possibility that it can show up in many different ways.

REM:
Repetition: Repeat as necessary to find your true desire.

Emotion: Neutrality wins the day. If you can stay neutral and open to the possibilities, the true feelings are easy to uncover.

Motion: No motion is necessary. Although it may be easier to think while you walk, exercise, or even journal.

Purpose:
By wanting something, you are telling the Universe that you are in lack, and this is what you are actually vibrating ... lack. The Universe will give you more of this lack *unless* you drop the want and identify exactly what your hopes and desires are—the feelings you are truly after.

Habits

Motivation is Internal

Let's say you have experienced 30 years of feeling down. Will one thought or one action change the feeling? Probably not. You are used to doing the same thing over and over. Don't worry—this is normal. It's become a habit. It's familiar. This is one reason habits are so hard to change—they're familiar.

The motivation to be different has to be internal (coming from within you) and stronger than the motivation to be the way you've always been. This motivation is then followed up with continuous actions that put you in the right direction—each making you one step closer to your intentions. Think of the actions as steps ... one foot in front of the other. You can step, tippy-toe, run, leap, or slither. But the idea is that you are doing something to move from where you are to where you desire to be.

When you do something over and over, your brain is making neural pathways. That's how it knows what to do. The neural pathways are the roads we have traveled. They are what feel comfortable. We all tend to do what is comfortable.

When we do something over and over, it becomes a habit because of the neural pathways in our brains. To do something different, you have to do that different thing over and over so that you can build new neural pathways and create a new habit. Some research says you have to do the new activity for 21 consecutive days to create a new habit.

The old pathways are still there, and they still feel comfortable. But as you use the new pathways more and more, they become the new comfortable.

Change Can Be Uncomfortable

The subconscious mind creates blocks to feeling good because we run on memorized patterns (habits), and most of our patterns are not about feeling good. We do what feels comfortable. Everything else causes us to react as if we are in danger.

Think about climbing a mountain. When we are at the bottom with our feet solidly on the ground, where we have always been, we are comfortable. But as we climb, we reach a point that's a little scary. Chances are we stop and take a breath until we feel comfortable. From this new feeling of comfortable, we continue the climb, stopping and re-acclimating as we need to until we finish. Once we have done it, it's not as scary, and we have a new pattern within our subconscious mind.

This is also true when we raise our children. At the beginning, we are handed the baby and have no clue what to do. We are in love with the baby, but we are frightened at the same time. But something happens as we progress through each phase. We become accustomed to it. We are more comfortable. And then it's on to the next phase where the cycle is repeated. In fact, this cycle continues as we age and approach the empty nest years. It's a cycle of new (causing fear) leading to familiarity (allowing comfort).

The same is true with feelings in the body. The body thinks that anything new is a prelude to disaster because it feels safe where it is ... the usual way of thinking, feeling, and doing. If it felt something different, then its survival would be threatened ... or at least the subconscious mind thinks so. By doing something new, we venture away from the familiar and comfortable, and the new experience leads us to a new feeling that can be frightening. It can feel as if we hit a wall and the body rebelled in some way, such as the stomach clutching, breathing interrupted, or a headache starting. But all the body is saying is, "I don't know how to handle this."

It makes sense to feel this way if the new thought is a very large, hungry tiger running towards you. But it doesn't make sense to run away from good feelings such as happiness, which many people do, because their bodies are rebelling if they do something too new. And recognizing the happiness that's already inside someone, but has been ignored for a lifetime, can be uncomfortable. So, the body tries to sabotage the happiness as a way to survive.

CHAPTER 14
Consciousness Concept Review

Habits

- ► When you do something over and over, your brain is making neural pathways. You are forming a habit based upon the road most often traveled in your brain.
- ► We tend to do what is comfortable. Everything else causes us to react as if we are in danger.
- ► To create a new habit (and new neural pathways), do the new activity for 21 consecutive days.
- ► We run on memorized patterns (habits).

Find The Good Exercise

How to do it:

1. Whenever something happens (even the bad stuff), ask yourself: What's good about this? How is this a benefit?
2. Repeat this as many times as needed until you can truly see that whatever happened could be a benefit for you in some way.

REM:

Repetition: The more good you look for, the more good you find.

Emotion: This exercise helps you move to a better feeling.

Motion: This can be done mentally, but writing will help you keep track of all the good that can come from it. It will also keep you on track, and you'll find more good because you won't give up as easily.

Purpose:

Your perspective and viewpoint change as you find the good. As a result, what seems bad doesn't seem so bad, and you will feel better about it. In fact, you will feel better overall. Shifting your focus from the supposedly negative to the positive allows you to focus on the good, thus helping you attract more good.

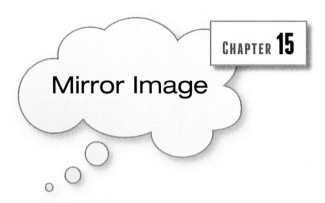

Mirror Image

The Outside World Reflects Your Inside Feelings

The world is a mirror. Whatever you are feeling on the inside is what you attract from the outside. Thus, if we are feeling love, respect, and kindness, then those are what we would be getting back ... experiences of love, respect, and kindness.

Have you ever noticed that when you feel truly great, your kids are nicer to you? And if they aren't, then their bad mood doesn't really bother you? And in general, good things just seem to happen? This is what it's like to be neutral and attract what you want in life.

However, if you happen to notice that your kids are yelling at you, being rude, slamming doors, etc. *and* it's bothering you, then chances are that you were feeling frustrated and angry *before* these things happened to you.

Often we think that the other people are "doing it to us," whereas in reality, we are doing it to ourselves. It is *because* we feel a certain way that people are reacting to us in the way they are.

Take a look at what is happening around you. Is your family in chaos? Before the chaos started, were you feeling focused and organized, *or* were you feeling chaotic within yourself? Or has the chaos been going on for so long that you can't imagine it any other way?

Is your family calm and polite as they talk? How are you feeling inside yourself? The calmer you feel, the calmer your experiences will be. (Yes, it is possible for you to feel one way and for your spouse to feel another way and have the kids react to each of you differently.)

To begin discovering what you are feeling, look at the outside world. What are the experiences you are attracting? What are the signs you notice? What thoughts keep appearing in your head? What do you keep saying? Pay attention.

Then say to yourself something along the lines of, "I wonder what I'm feeling on the inside to attract this _____ (event)." Let it go. Don't worry about the answer. It will come to you. It will come to you in a minute, an hour, a day ... eventually. The more you notice, the clearer things will get. And the clearer they get, the more you will notice.

I had one experience recently with JT, my oldest son. I asked him a question that required some thinking and juggling of schedules. He very calmly asked me, "Could we talk about this some other time? I have a horrible headache." This shocked me. He'd never asked me in such a nice way before. He was calm and respectful. I responded likewise. "Of course. And thank you for asking me. It's much better than being yelled at." We both left the experience feeling good. I must have been running good energy to attract this. (It also helps that he's 25 and is figuring out this communication stuff. But the change only happened recently, so I'm still in shock.)

If you don't like what you are attracting, change your feelings. Change how you feel on the inside. Then watch as your reality shifts. Reality is only what you think is real. It's not what is actually real. It's only true until it's not. We are each attracting our own reality.

Make an Attitude Adjustment

Make an attitude adjustment. Adjust **your own** attitude—then the world will line up to give you what you are feeling. After all, you can't change others...you can only change yourself. However, as you change yourself, others will change in response to how you've changed.

As I sat in my office writing this chapter, I asked myself, "I wonder what more I could write about the world being a mirror." The Universe answered. I could hear JT screaming, "*Women f*** everything up.*" What? As it turns out, he was watching a TV show and didn't like whatever was happening. But what he screamed (with lots of emotion) was an eye opener for me. In that moment in time, he felt this. It became obvious to me that for as long as he felt this, he wouldn't be having a great relationship with a woman, which is something he truly desires. (He tends to pick girls with lots of drama. Remember the bit about habit? His sister was a lot of drama, and this became normal and comfortable for him, so that's what he subconsciously is attracted to.)

His life (no girlfriend at the moment) is mirroring something he is thinking and feeling—women screw everything up. Does he have to know where it came from? No. It might be interesting, but he doesn't have to know. All he has to do is decide that he wants something different—a better feeling.

As a parent, I could have run to him and given him a lecture about how women should be valued and cherished, treated with respect, etc. But I didn't. He was obviously expressing a deep feeling that was a reaction to something that happened in his life previously. (It was at this point that I remembered that his last girlfriend was physically abusive. Luckily, he was smart enough to walk away from the fight and the relationship.)

My boyfriend did go in the room to check to make sure everything was all right and that it wasn't something more than the TV. This topic will come up for conversation in the future ... probably multiple times. But in the heat of the moment, I don't have to attack him. I don't have to tell him how he is wrong or how to change it. I can let him feel whatever he is feeling.

At a later date, when we are both calm, we will be discussing this. But I'll probably wait until he brings up the issue of finding a girlfriend. (Or until he reads this book.)

Follow the Signs

Immediately, the Universe will be putting signs (answers to your questions) in your path. Stay on the lookout for them. Then follow these signs to the positive actions that will help you achieve your intentions.

Now, think of your teens as they navigate the relationships they have. They are forming the rules they will have about relationships *on top of* the rules they have absorbed while observing you and others. The choices they make now may affect them in the future. But don't worry ... they are just figuring it out. They can always make new choices. The clue is to talk with them (and yourself) about choices and paying attention to the signs that show up in their lives.

Adam is beginning a new relationship with himself as he looks at colleges. Recently he told me that while he was looking at college brochures, he got a headache looking at one in particular. When he put it down and looked at the brochure of the school he "knows" he will be going to, the headache went away. He listened to the sign (the headache) and took action (put the brochure down and stopped looking at that school). He reevaluated (looked at the other school) and felt the sign (no headache). He was smart enough to recognize the sign, pay attention to it, and take different action. It wasn't necessary for him to figure out why. All he had to do was follow his feelings and look for what felt better.

Part of the reason he listened to the sign is that his family values this and supports him in doing so. (If you grow up with someone telling you to listen to your head/mind instead of heart/feelings, you learn to not value your gut feelings.) Out of all my kids, he's the one that has been with me the longest (living under the same roof) as I've learned to listen to myself, so he's just naturally absorbed it.

My oldest daughter, Bethany, must have absorbed some of the value of listening to the heart even though she was pretty much out of the house when I first started learning how to do so. When she had her baby, she and her husband asked the baby, "Is your name Makenna?" The baby cried. Then she asked, "Is your name Morgan?" The baby stopped crying and was happy. Wow! They were letting their daughter pick her own name! They paid attention to the sign. (And more than that, they thought to ask the questions.)

But what if the signs are too abstract or you don't trust what you are seeing or feeling? Set an intention and say a prayer or ask the angels to show you a sign. But in some way, outline how you'll know when you've got it.

Since so many people are looking for their "perfect mate," let's use that as an example. Start by writing down everything that you hope for in a mate. When I did this, I wrote six pages (or was it nine?) about what I desired in a mate. Even I recognized that the list was just a little bit too long. Did it really matter if he wore button-down shirts with the sleeves rolled up to the elbows?

So the next step was to narrow down the list to the top 10 qualifications. From there, narrow it further, if possible, to the top five. Try bunching together the qualifications into groups by finding the common denominators. You'll notice that when you get done with this list, what's left is most likely the feelings that the "things" on your list would give you.

For example, what the rolled up sleeves really meant for me was relaxed security (vs. uptight security). Rolled up sleeves were security? Sure. In my experience, men who worked hard rolled their sleeves up and were successful. This doesn't mean men in short sleeved shirts don't work hard and aren't successful, but my symbol (rolled up sleeves) is based on my past experiences. And relaxed is always more attractive to me than uptight and tense. And besides, I think it looks sexy.

By looking at all the qualifying "things" and bunching them together, I'm actually able to include more of them by going to the feeling that I really desire.

From feeling these feelings, try writing a series of letters to the person. Pretend you have already met him and are having a conversation with him through letters.

I did this and wrote for a few weeks every night before bed. (By the way, whatever you do right before bed is what your subconscious mind works on while you are sleeping.) I included, "I'll know you because …"

Then I put the journal away when it felt complete (translation: when I lost interest in writing any more) and forgot about it … for a year and a half, until while looking for something else, I ran across this "lost" journal. I opened it and read, "I'll know you because you make me a better me." This wasn't my normal way of talking, and I'd actually said this to my current boyfriend, whom I'd only known for one month at that point! I shocked myself.

But by finding the journal, I reminded myself of the sign I'd set up to know when I'd found him. Past signs (to recognize previous boyfriends) I set up for myself were that he'd wear orange. (That perfect-at-the-time boyfriend loved the color orange.) Next, I chose purple (and that boyfriend loved the color purple). Or the time I was conflicted about breaking up with the purple-loving boyfriend, I asked the angels to give me a sign that was so big I'd have to trip over it. The next morning, my doctor (who is a friend) said, "The only thing wrong with you is that you have to break up with your boyfriend. The emotions are hurting you. I wasn't planning on saying that—it just came out."

As you can see, you can set up the signs yourself (orange, purple, asking the angels for a big sign, a certain phrase, etc.) or you can just interpret the signs that are already there. It's up to you. It's your life, and you get to choose.

I know the example above wasn't teen related, but the same theory applies. You are looking for a relationship with your teen. Outline what a good relationship will look like. Then pretend that you have already met this teen and write letters to him. Or pretend that you know he is coming in the future, and you are so excited to meet him. Again, write him letters. By focusing on the good, you will attract more good.

Sometimes what we get isn't what we think we asked for. A client of mine wanted more time with her three girls. Well, when the girls got lice, she got to spend a lot of time with them. Luckily, she could laugh it off and not get upset. She could enjoy the time they did have together.

Be open to what shows up and trust that it's perfect. Even if you can't see the perfection, trust that in some unknown way, it will be perfect for you.

Timing of the Universe

The Universe has its own timing … and it isn't always the timing we'd like. Think of a baby. We know that a pregnancy is usually 40 weeks from the last cycle—which, by the way, is actually ten months not nine. But if you want to get technical, conception is usually two weeks into the cycle, so the actual pregnancy is 38 weeks. However, some babies are "done cooking" before this, and some take longer. It's not up to us to decide exactly when the baby will arrive. And for that matter, some babies come out very quickly, and others take a loooong time. As I wrote this, I was waiting for my first grandchild to arrive. I could have gotten the call that night or in three weeks. But until then, we waited.

If you have the belief/rule that *things will work out*, then the wait is easier. If you instead have the rule that *nothing works out*, then the wait is more tense and more uncomfortable. It might work out, or it might not. But either way, you are vibrating with your beliefs. So as you sit back and observe what is happening (notice I didn't say you were trying to make anything happen, you are just observing), which rule do you think will be easier to live with?

Yes, I know that your experiences in the past influence your feelings now, but are you living in the past? Or is this experience in this moment? And for that matter, is the experience actually you, or is it just something that you are experiencing? We don't actually have to collect and hold onto all of our past experiences. We can let them go, even if it's only to grab onto the new ones before us.

Imagine climbing a tree. Each time you reach for the next higher branch, you have to let go of the one you are on. You can't hold onto all the branches at the same time. Now, if you were ten years old, you would be able to climb almost any tree (providing you have the basic skills necessary) ... as long as the tree was mature enough. Even a ten year old can't climb a sapling—the timing isn't right. However, if that child wanted to climb a specific sapling, he would have to wait until the tree was grown up enough ... tall and strong enough to hold the child's weight. But does that mean that the child can't do anything in the meantime? No. Does the child have to rant and rave that the tree isn't growing fast enough? No. The child can live a full life and climb many other trees while waiting for the tree to grow. After all, the tree has it's own timing, and the child has a choice to go along with it or fight against it and try to control it ... however, the tree is going to grow at its own pace no matter what the child does.

In fact, everything has its own timing. Once you learn to let go of trying to control the timing, life is actually much more peaceful. Be an observer and watch what goes on around you. If something is taking longer than expected, try saying something like, *"Oh good. Can it get even better? I don't have to know how or even when ... I just have to know that it's coming."*

Do you see that what you tell yourself influences how you feel while you are waiting? Sometimes we know why things are delayed, but other times, we don't. Trust in the Universe that *the timing will be perfect,* even if the outcome is different from what you thought it would be.

If the Universe has a pot of gold for you, but in your head you can only get it once you are 30, but it shows up at 28, are you going to turn it down just because the timing is different from what you set up? Or are you going to be angry with the Universe if it doesn't show up until you are 52? Maybe the Universe is waiting for you to do something specific before it can act and give you the pot of gold.

CHAPTER **15**

Consciousness Concept Review

Mirror Image/Attitude Adjustment/Signs/Timing

▶ Often we think that the other people are "doing it to us," whereas in reality, we are doing it to ourselves.

▶ The more you notice, the clearer things will get. And the clearer they get, the more you will notice.

▶ Make an attitude adjustment. Adjust your own attitude.

▶ Every time you make a connection with a sign, it touches the memory of the feeling that you associate with it.

▶ Sometimes what we get isn't what we think we asked for.

▶ Be open to the possibility that what shows up is even better than what you expected.

▶ Is the experience actually you, or is it just something that you are experiencing?

▶ Everything has its own timing. Trust in the Universe that the timing will be perfect, even if the outcome is different from what you thought it would be.

Dear Future _____ Journal Exercise

How to do it:

1. Choose nice paper or a journal to record your letters to your future relationship (with your teenager, romantic partner, yourself, job, money, or any other relationship). It is possible to type out the journal, but don't get too caught up in correcting your spelling and grammar as you go along. This will inhibit your ideas and feelings from flowing.

2. Before bed (or first thing in the morning), set aside some time.

3. Write: Dear Future _____.

4. Then write a letter to this future relationship.

5. Tell the relationship about yourself.

6. Ask questions of the "person" as if you were really going to give him the letter.

7. Talk about the improvements you will see, or the good that will happen. (You can also write as if it's already happened.)

8. Remember to stay in the good you see coming your way. You can complain ... if you want more complaining in your life. I recommend staying in the good.

REM:

Repetition: Do a series of letters, each one expressing more of your desires.

Emotion: Open your heart and write as if you are feeling love toward this relationship.

Motion: Writing is a motion, especially writing by hand.

Purpose:

Dear Future _____ letters help you to find the good that will be waiting for you. It helps to set your intentions on the good.

Happiness

Happiness is a Choice

Most people are stuck in unhappiness, not realizing that happiness is a choice—one that they can make. Luckily, it's just a habit. And as with any habit, it can be changed. You don't have to wait for something to happen. Joy and happiness are only a decision away.

I had to decide which road I wanted to travel—happy or unhappy. When I chose happiness, I went all out and even changed my name to Joy. I can keep telling myself that; but in reality, I got divorced and wanted to make up my own name. (Going back to my maiden name felt like I was moving backwards.) I tried all sorts of names, but it wasn't until I started to notice the signs the Universe was giving me (Joy kept popping up in articles, book titles, conversations, etc.) that I knew what name was calling out to me. It made me happy, so I went with it.

Once I set the goal and decided on joy, the next step was to decide what happiness and joy *looked like.* I needed a visual, so I created a vision board. I started with a lot of magazines. I cut out any pictures or words that made me feel good. Feeling good is a very important component of being happy. I then pasted the pictures and words on a large poster board. It wasn't intentional, but they fell into three categories: peace, laughter, and connection. My vision board was filled with peaceful scenes, people laughing, and people connecting in positive ways such as dancing. Every time I looked at the vision board, I felt a sense of peace. I didn't worry about how I was going to "get" what was on the board. I just felt happy.

For me, happiness and joy felt like feeling good through peace, laughter, and connection. What does happiness mean for you? How do you recognize joy and happiness? Take a look at the following chart for some examples of what happiness and unhappiness look like.

UNHAPPINESS	HAPPINESS
Pessimistic (everything as bad)	Optimistic (a positive outlook on life)
Critical of self and others	Appreciate and accept self and others
Negative thoughts, expectations, and actions (anger, depression, resentment, fear, worry, etc.)	Positive thoughts, expectations and actions (laughter, a sense of fulfillment, tranquility, etc.)
An attitude of taking	An attitude of giving
No real direction	Having purpose and meaning in life
Life is a chore.	Life is an adventure.
You have no control over your life.	You own your own time and have a sense of control.
The feeling you are all alone in the universe	A belief that there is something bigger than you
A sense of disconnection	A sense of connection

One of the exercises that I did to move from unhappiness to happiness was to ask myself if I can be happy anyway when something isn't going my way. It's a very simple question that means a great deal. *Even though xyz is happening, could I be happy anyway?* I'm not saying I *will* be happy, only that I can allow myself and give myself permission to be happy.

Along the way, I found out that when I became happier, I also had the characteristics on the happiness side of the chart. Or did I have them and then became happier? It doesn't matter—I'm just happy to be happy.

Shortcuts to Happiness

To feel more comfortable about happiness (love, peace, etc.), try a shortcut to deal directly with the feeling and look for things that make you happy.

Shortcut 1: Notice how you feel. Ask yourself, "Is it okay to feel as _____ (happy, good, loving, etc.) as I am right now?" Then follow with "Is it okay to feel better than this?" Keep asking if it's okay to feel even better. When you "hit the wall" and feel the panic, do a quick hand balancing (old feeling—new feeling). Then continue with, "Is it okay to feel as _____ (happy, good, loving, etc.) as I am right now?"

Shortcut 2: Hang out with people who are the way you desire to feel. Isn't it easier to be happy when you are with happy people instead of sad people?

Remember how your parents were so concerned about who your friends were as you grew up? It's still true even as adults. So now make the conscious decision to be friends with the people you admire and hope to be like.

So, when you get together with other parents, what are you talking about? Are you complaining about or complimenting your teen? What are the other parents talking about? It's easy to get sucked into complaining if that's what everyone else is doing. However, if you are neutral, then you can let the complaints drift away, without you participating in them. You can talk about all the good stuff your teen is doing. (Remember, what you focus on is what you get. If you focus on the good stuff your teen is doing, then more good stuff will happen.) And you may notice along the way that you don't want to converse with the people who are always complaining. That's okay—chances are they don't want to hear all the good stuff you're sharing. It's okay to find new friends who are more in line with how you are now that you are noticing the good.

Shortcut 3: Look for things that make you happy, then do them. Sometimes we do things only because they are familiar. But if we shed the familiar and try something new, we may find we like something else. It may be something small like taking a walk, or it may be something big like going back to school to learn something you love.

Shortcut 4: Be an observer. Are you the feeling? Or is the feeling something you are experiencing? Does the feeling define who you are? Is it okay to let go of that feeling?

Once we truly observe our feelings (instead of letting them run our lives), the feeling loses some of its "oomph". The feeling becomes less important. This is actually something you will discover as you do the possibility thinking and hand balancing too. Observing a feeling and remembering that the feeling isn't you—it's just something you are experiencing in the moment—will happen more often. And you will notice that the things that used to bother you stop bothering you. *The more you observe and witness, the better you feel.*

Step back and observe what is going on. Then say to yourself, "Hmmm. That's interesting. I wonder how that will benefit me." This puts you in the witnessing mode and has you starting to look for the benefit, which is also called the gold.

Shortcut 5: Say, "I'm living my dream!" when people ask you how you are doing. And then follow it up with all the good in your life. This will remind you of the good, help you focus on it, and thus allow you to feel even better.

Often when people respond to, "How are you?" they respond in the negative and list all the things that are wrong in their lives. Turn it on its head. It's not a contest to see who has the most things wrong—be the one to start the trend to notice the good. Notice the good in your life, then talk about it. Say thank you for it. Remember ... the more attention you give something, the more it grows.

And as an added bonus, people won't know how to respond because they are used to the litany of bad. Be the leader and lead your friends one by one to terrific talk. Notice the good in their lives as well as the good in your life. Look for all the good stuff. That's the gold. And I don't just mean the material things. Look for the simple things like a smile or being able to trust someone. Complimenting your friends will actually make you, as well as your friends, feel good. And as a side benefit, the more you find to compliment, the more compliments will find their way to you. But remember that *new feelings take time to acclimate to.* It's a new feeling, and the neural pathways are just forming. *Just give it a chance and balance.*

CHAPTER 16
Consciousness Concept Review

Happiness

▶ Happiness is a choice.

▶ Is it okay to feel whatever I feel right now?

▶ Associate with people who feel the way you desire to feel.

▶ Do something that allows you to feel better.

▶ Observe your feelings. You aren't the feeling.

▶ "I'm living my dream." Focus on the good.

Vision Board Exercise

How to do it:

1. Collect magazines, books, cartoons, etc. that can be cut up. If you like to draw, you may draw the images, or you can collect them from the computer.
2. Cut out words and pictures that are exactly what you hope for or are somehow representative of your desires.
3. Put the words and pictures on poster board. The organization is up to you. Follow your instincts. They can be glued on the board. They can be loose so that you can move them around to "see" new connections.
4. Hang the vision board on the wall (if pictures are glued on) or put it on a table (if loose).

REM:

Repetition: You see it over and over and keep reminding yourself of where you are headed.

Emotion: Choose those things that have the feelings you are striving for with this vision board. Every time you see it, you remind yourself of the feelings and thus feel them before they arrive.

Motion: The act of looking, cutting, and applying the pictures and words makes them one step closer to reality.

Purpose:

Picture what you desire to have, do, or be and then get/follow/have that knowing feeling, the feeling of certainty that it will happen.

Truth

It's Only True Until It's Not

When you believe something, you think it is true, and you create your life around this truth. You trust that what you believe to be true is in fact true. However, *"It's only true until it's not."* We only think something is true; and because we think it to be true, it is ... until our thoughts change. Then a new truth is born.

Everyone used to think the world was flat, but then they "discovered" that it's round. What if, in the future, this truth is challenged? Right now, we believe the earth is a solid, round shape. We even have pictures to prove it. But what if science advances in some direction, and we find out the earth is some other shape ... maybe finding out that it literally pulses with energy and this pulsing can be seen? Or what if the world dematerialized and then rematerialized every nanosecond, and this was the pulse? It would certainly change our beliefs and what we trust to be true.

When we believe something to be true, we create our reality around this belief. But what if what I believe to be true is different from what you believe to be true? That's okay. Everyone is living in their own reality, which is actually a reflection of their own thoughts and feelings. And when a lot of people believe the same thing, a morphic field is formed. This tends to have a stronger impact because so many people believe it. But that also falls prey to *"It's only true until it's not."*

Take the beliefs around a disease. People believe the disease is incurable until a cure is found. But what many people don't look at is why did they get the disease in the first place? What is out of sync in their thoughts and feelings that would attract the disease? Where and why is the energy stuck? What's good about having this disease?

The important point here is that your thoughts and then your feelings about those thoughts vibrate out into the world and attract your experiences to you. If you want to change what you attract to you, then you need to change your beliefs, thoughts, and feelings. Your vibrations will change, and then you will attract different results.

Rules Are True ... Until They Aren't

Our thoughts are reflected in the rules we live our lives by. Rules are statements of truth ... as we *believe* them to be true. This doesn't mean they are true. We only believe that they are. To move from a statement, we must first ask, "Is this rule working for you?" Notice that we asked a question. The question allows movement and allows for something else to come in. It's not an either/or. It's not polarity. A question allows for something even better.

Sometimes the rules that we adopt can be changed in a single moment. I once had the rule that *if I went to bed after midnight, then I'd wake up with a headache.* The Universe was giving me what I was expecting. If I went to bed at 11:59, chances were I'd wake up without a headache. But if I went to bed at 12:01 (only two minutes later), I'd wake up with a headache. It eventually dawned on me how silly it was.

So, on the spot, I decided (notice I made a decision) that this wasn't working for me. I needed to believe something different. I said, "New Rule" and then mentally ran through some possible new rules, such as: *Sleep is restful and rejuvenating. Upon awaking, I feel alive and great. The time I go to bed has no influence on how my head feels when I wake up.*

The whole process can be as easy as recognizing the rule, asking if it's working for you (how is it showing up in your life?), and saying "New Rule," then making up a new rule. You don't have to do all the emotional balancing and possibility thinking.

However, many rules have multiple layers. One rule can show up in many areas of your life. So while you think you are changing THE rule, you may be in fact only changing part of it, because you didn't recognize the deeper belief at play. When you ask yourself what all of these experiences in your life have in common, you will be closer to finding the deeper belief at play.

Think of a dandelion. It's there, and then you "make up a rule" that it's not there because you cut off the visible part. However, the taproot (the part that is really deep in the ground) is still there, and another dandelion will grow above the surface. To truly remove the dandelion, you must dig out the taproot.

Of course you can always use weed killer, but the side effects of the poison affect more than just the dandelion. It goes into the ground and eventually into the water table below the ground—which, by the way, is the same water we drink. These are what I call unintended consequences. If you are spraying one dandelion, it doesn't seem to be that big of a deal. But if everyone sprays entire yards, then it is a big deal.

So, if we dig deep and find the taproot of our rules, then they will neutralize, and we can make up the rules that do work for us.

The dandelion equals how the rule shows up.

Cutting the dandelion is the first new rule.

The taproot is what the deeper belief is.

Digging it out is the balancing, allowing for new possibilities and making a new rule.

Weed killer is all of the coping mechanisms—such as drugs—that seem to do a good job, but really only take care of the symptoms, not the root cause of the problem. They also have unintended consequences or side effects. (As a side note, there is no such thing as a side effect. They are all effects. Not everyone gets every effect.)

A new rule is only a decision away. Begin by saying, "New Rule." It's that simple. You have already decided that the old rule wasn't working for you, and you are willing to make up a new one. If it's an easy rule to change, you can just think up a new rule that will work for you. Make it as broad as possible.

Personally, I prefer that the new rules don't start with "I." It seems egocentric; and if everything starts with "I," then they are harder to remember. However, some rules do start with "I." It's not a hard and fast rule; but if I take the time to play with the wording, something better usually comes up.

When I was learning Matrix Energetics, one of the teachers had the rule that *change is useful or nothing happens*. When we are talking about shifting energy and allowing new possibilities, this covers the possibility that whatever I do will not cause harm. I liked it and adopted it. It has worked for me. Even if something looks bad initially, I know that the change is useful in some way. I don't have to know *how*, just that it is.

So when you make up a new rule (preferably after balancing the energy and feeling neutral), ask yourself what it is that you would like to happen. Ask yourself a series of questions. Here are a few sample ones:

- ▶ What if it were different?
- ▶ Could I allow it to be better?
- ▶ Does this rule feel true?
- ▶ Does some part of the rule want to shift?
- ▶ Could I allow a different rule?
- ▶ How can this rule show up in my life?
- ▶ What are more possibilities?
- ▶ Is there a better way of saying the rule?

When you hit upon the right rule, you will know it. It will literally give you a feeling in your body. It's an ahh feeling. Mentally you'll say, "*Of course this is it. It just feels right.*"

If the rule is broad enough, it will affect many areas of your life, and you will rapidly see things change. If the rule is narrow, some things will change.

Warning: Once you adopt the new rule, the Universe may bring up some of the experiences from the old rule as if it's asking, "Are you sure you want to change? Here's a chance to stay how you've always been." The simple solution is to repeat the new rule and step forward with confidence into your "new" habits.

Talking about habits, you may need to repeat the new rule over and over to remind yourself of it. Don't get all down in the dumps about it—just make it a game. When the old rule pops up, laugh and say something like, "That's the old rule. My new rule is ..." As with anything, the more times you repeat it, the stronger it gets.

One of my tricks is that I write some of the rules on index cards and post them on my bulletin board where I can see them every time I sit at my desk. This gives me repetition. When my boyfriend came into my office and looked at my rules, he laughed at two rules in particular. *This or something better.* And

I expect the best. I get the best. He's thinking of jewelry (and I do have some very nice jewelry, but not the best by a long shot ... just the best for me). I'm thinking, I have him in my life. He's the best. *I only need the best for me.*

For someone else, their rule may guide them to *"give the best"* or something about *"the best for everyone around them"* or *"best for society as a whole."* Your rules don't have to work for everyone else. They only have to work for you.

Not every rule has to be perfect. If you make a rule and decide to change it again, change it. After all, it's your life, and you can make the rules that work for you and give you the life you desire. Your rules and the attached feelings determine the experiences you attract. These experiences are your life.

Changing your rules may change your life in unexpected ways. Just be aware that when you make up a new rule, it will change the experiences that you attract.

If you have the rule that I do about expecting the best and having the best, then one opportunity that may come for you is to "take" or "steal" something so that you have the best. Is this what you really want? What is your definition of "the best"? Do you want the best at the expense of hurting others or doing something that much of society thinks is wrong? Do you want to take something that clearly doesn't belong to you? Do you want to feel entitled to something? Do you want to feel the guilt that goes along with it? Do you want to feel as if you have to be on the lookout for someone coming after you? Do you want to feel that you've earned it? Do you want to feel ... there are many different variations of how you may feel.

Personally, I'm not into taking and stealing. This goes against my grain, because I have a stronger rule that says, *"I'm honest and trustworthy."* But do you see that the combination of the two rules (best and honest) will have a different effect than if the "best" was paired up with *"I'm entitled to have whatever you have."* (Be careful about your rules. If you have the rule *"I'm entitled to have whatever you have,"* it may show up as the trouble, disease, or other bad stuff that the other person has.)

Finding Your Limiting Beliefs

The question is, "How do we identify what our limiting beliefs are?" The simple answer is to open your eyes, ears, mind, and heart to what is already there. It is sort of like a mystery tour of your subconscious mind—the part of the mind that you aren't aware of. You see it so often that you no longer see it. Looking at the obvious can be more difficult than looking at something brand new. Look at everything around you. Look at what you say. Pay attention to what you read. Pay attention to what other people say that you agree (and disagree) with. Pay attention to the commercials, TV shows, movies, billboards, books, and so on, that attract your attention. The act of attracting your attention is the Universe telling you, "Pay attention. This is important to you."

For an indication of some of your beliefs, take a look at the t-shirts and bumper stickers around you. Do you really want these sayings to be your reality? *"Next mood swing, 6 minutes,"* *"I don't do mornings,"* or *"A husband is the only one of your children that doesn't grow up and move away."* You can see that while these may be humorous, you probably don't want them to come true in your life. Yet, by reading the belief, saying it, and wearing it every time you wear the t-shirt, you are attracting the belief into your reality. In fact, a single limiting belief is probably showing up in many areas of your life in many different ways.

So, now that you have identified a limiting belief, what do you do about it? The first thing is to stop saying it. Even stop thinking it if you can. At least you won't be perpetuating it. The second thing is to let it go. "Could I allow myself to let go of (whatever the belief is)?" This question may have to be repeated until you actually believe it.

One way to change a limiting belief is to change your point of view and look for the belief that would fit with the life you choose to live. Replace the limiting belief with what you want the new belief to be. State it in the positive and treat it as if it already exists (versus something in the future, which by design must always stay in the future, so you'll never have it). Remember the bit about "If it was possible, could I allow (state the reality you would like to see happen)?" Use this question to help you form the feelings and reality that you do want to bring into your life.

Pay attention to your body. Your body gives you clues. Every ache and pain you get has an emotional component to it. For example, lungs are associated with fear. The liver is associated with anger. The right side of the body is associated with the male energy such as career. The left side of the body is associated with female energy such as nurturing. The list goes on. There are many great lists associating parts of the body with certain emotions. (For a good one, see Louise Hay's *Heal Your Body*)

The general rule of thumb I've found is to ask a question about the body part. For example, if your stomach hurts, ask "What is eating at you?" or "What can't you digest?" If it hurts to breathe, ask "What takes your breath away?" or "What causes you to gasp?" If your knee hurts, ask "What am I being inflexible about?" or "Why am I afraid to move forward?" Use your intuition to determine what the questions should be. It's okay to ask more than one question. It's okay to say, "No, that's not it." or "Yes, that feels right." Trust your intuition.

Warning: Sometimes we want the answer to be something, when in fact, it is something else altogether. It may even be the opposite of what we think it should be. If you uncover the

*feeling about the answer to your question, balance out the energy
around that thought/feeling. Then if the pain changes, you are in
fact on the right track. Sometimes the change is instantaneous.
Other times, you have to dig and dig and dig before the physical
energy shifts and you feel better.*

(As a side note, it's okay to get some physical relief for your
symptoms as long as you look for the root cause and shift the
energy. If you only take the medicine for the headache, but
never look at what emotions are causing the headaches, then
you are going to keep getting more headaches. Your body is
trying to tell you something. It's up to you to listen.)

Underlying Beliefs Determine Your Rules

We make up our rules to support our underlying, limiting
beliefs that we have told ourselves, which originated from our
perceptions. If we were to take all (or at least a whole bunch) of
the rules we made up about ourselves, they would usually stem
from just a few underlying, limiting beliefs.

Example underlying, limiting beliefs are:

- I'm not worthy.
- I'm not desirable.
- I'm not loveable.
- Etc.

We make up our rules to support the underlying beliefs. For
example, if my underlying belief is that I'm not desirable, then
I'll set up the rules in my life (unconsciously of course) to make
sure that I keep proving this to myself. I may choose hairstyles,
clothes, etc. that aren't flattering. I may even walk with my head
down and my shoulders up to "hide" who I am, because if I

think I'm undesirable, I can't appear desirable. I may not even desire myself (which is usually at the bottom of the belief).

For example, if someone chooses to be an artist, but believes he is undesirable, he may make up a false rule that says *no one wants to buy (no one desires) my paintings*. This of course leads to him putting out the vibration that matches this. The result is that his vibration pushes away the buyers, no one buys the paintings, and he gets to tell himself (subconsciously), "*My paintings aren't desirable, therefore I'm not desirable.*"

Many people think that the action comes before the feeling … he doesn't sell the paintings so he develops the feeling that no one desires his paintings (and by extension, him). And after a life-time of the action, one can certainly see how the rules he's made for himself have been enforced, and thus have a lot of power.

But what if the very first time he felt he was undesirable had nothing to do with his art abilities? What if it was as simple as he showed his mom and dad something he did that he was proud of, but at that moment they were fighting? The reaction the little boy received was being yelled at for "interrupting" and "both-ering" his parents. (A different kid might not even be affected by all of this. The emotions of the moment may have no effect on him, or he may have the confidence in himself that he just knows his project is good regardless of what others say or do. Or he sets up a rule to "prove himself" to the world.)

As adults, we can see that the parents probably don't mean to belittle the boy. The fight may not even have anything to do with him. The issue is really about them. But in the strong emo-tions of the moment, perhaps the boy decided to believe that *he was undesirable.* Or this was the final straw, and he'd had other brief moments of thinking he was undesirable—this just cemented it for him. From there, he made up rules such as, "*I can't do anything right. I'm a bother. No one is interested in me.*"

And so on. Then he lives his life proving these rules to be true. He may not actually think he is trying to prove himself correct, because he doesn't actually like the feelings. But the Universe only wants him to be happy; and if he's thinking and feeling the rules, then that must be what he desires, so the Universe will bring experiences to him to prove him right. In other words, he is attracting what he's vibrating.

Sometimes the rules go so far as to say that *I'll die if* _____ *(I'm desired, loved, etc.)*. Or *I'll die if* _____ *(x happens or x doesn't happen)*. These rules set up a cycle of fear, and the emotions surrounding the "I'll die" statements are very strong. In order to survive, whatever it is must be avoided at all costs. It's truly a matter of survival . . . at least in his mind it is.

A rule or belief leads to certain thoughts, feelings, and actions, which may or may not work out for a person; but who the person *could* have been changes based upon the rules he tells himself. His life force or innate gifts don't develop as he attracts experiences into his life to "prove himself right." He's at a fork in the road and doesn't even know it. He starts to cover up his unconditioned self by making up false rules to support his limiting beliefs.

Let's look at a simple example. Imagine being able to turn right and left at a moment's thought. Then for some reason, you've made up a rule that turning left is dangerous, so you no longer turn left. Instead, you only turn right or go straight. To go to the really great store (which is to the left of you), you will have to take more actions (multiple right turns). Or you may decide, "I don't really need to go there. I'll go somewhere else." Can you see how a simple decision can change your course of action and even the outcome? It can even change your life. What if the store on the left was your true desire and purpose in life, yet you couldn't turn left to get there?

CHAPTER 17
Consciousness Concept Review

Truth/New Rule/Limiting Beliefs

▶ We only think something is true; and because we think it to be true, it is ... until our thoughts change.

▶ When we believe something to be true, we create our reality around this belief.

▶ If you want to change what you attract to you, then you need to change your beliefs, thoughts, and feelings.

▶ Rules are statements of truth ... as we believe them to be true. This doesn't mean they are true. We only believe that they are.

▶ One rule can show up in many areas of your life.

▶ A new rule is only a decision away.

▶ Changing your rules may change your life in unexpected ways. Be aware that when you make up a new rule, it will change the experiences that you attract.

▶ To identify limiting beliefs, open your eyes, ears, mind, and heart to what is already showing up in your life. Pay attention to what you have attracted.

▶ State the new belief in the positive and treat it as if it already exists.

▶ Sometimes the rules go so far as to say, "I'll die if _____ happens or doesn't happen."

▶ A rule (belief) leads to thoughts, feelings, and actions, which may or may not work out for you. But who you *could* have been changes based upon the rules you tell yourself.

New Rule Exercise

How to do it:

1. Begin by paying attention to your thoughts, feelings, and words.
2. Look at what you are attracting in your life and look for the common themes between what you are attracting. Look for repeating patterns.
3. Ask yourself, "Is this working for me?" If yes, you don't need to change anything. If no, then you can say, "New Rule!"
4. Ask yourself a series of questions to help you uncover a new rule that will work for you.
   a. What if it were different?
   b. Could I allow it to be better?
   c. Does this rule feel true?
   d. Does some part of the rule want to shift?
   e. Could I allow a different rule?
   f. How can this rule show up in my life?
   g. Do I like the possibilities?
   h. Is there a better way of saying the rule?
   i. What was my part in this?
   j. If I had a feeling underneath this want, what might my true desire be?
   k. Even though _____, could I feel great anyway?
   l. I wonder how many ways _____?
   m. I wonder how this can be different?
   n. I wonder if it can be better than that?
   o. What is my habit?
   p. Is it okay to feel as good as I might right now?
   q. Am I the feeling, or am I observing what shows up?
   r. What's interesting about this?
   s. How will that benefit me?

5. From the questions, new thoughts will flow.

6. Make up a new rule that will benefit you. Test it out. If it works, keep it. If it doesn't, change the rule.

REM:

Repetition: This is an ongoing process. You can look at everything in your life and change the rules.

Emotion: Stay in a wondering "wow," or "that's interesting" frame of mind. This helps you be an observer and not a judge.

Motion: This is something good to do while your body is occupied with movement such as walking, biking, or running, as it will help new ideas to flow.

Purpose:

Staying in a questioning frame of mind will open the doors to something different showing up. Doing so will help you find the rules that work for and benefit you.

Reality

Reality is an Observation

Reality is only a reality based upon your perception as seen through the rules you live your life by. Reality is what is true for each of us. A trick is to be a true observer in your own life. This allows you to ask, "Is it me? Is the experience me, or is it just something I'm experiencing?"

Imagine putting on your shirt and pants when you get dressed in the morning. You are experiencing the clothing, but is the clothing you? Of course not. Well, the same is true of our bodies. Imagine a spirit, the essence of whom you are on the highest level, moving into a body for a lifetime. The body becomes like clothing for the spirit. But is the body the spirit? Or is the body something the spirit is experiencing? Now imagine the emotions the spirit experiences ... anger, happiness, sadness, and so on. Are the emotions the spirit? No. They are just something the spirit is experiencing.

From the spirit's perspective, it's experiencing all of this, and as such is observing or witnessing what it is experiencing. This is an important point. All of these experiences are just that ... experiences. They aren't the spirit. The spirit is witnessing the experiences.

They are just experiences the spirit is choosing to participate in. Whatever the spirit feels or senses is its reaction to the experience. It can choose to be offended, like it, or ignore it. But at the core, it is the spirit's choice. It is in control. It's not giving up control; it's just making a choice.

So how does this apply to you? Substitute spirit for you. You are the spirit living in your body. Your spirit has chosen your body to live in for this lifetime and chooses to experience what you experience.

Pain as an Attention Getter

Isn't this great! Once you look at things in this manner, life becomes much easier. The headache that I had yesterday? It's just something my spirit is choosing to experience. How I react to it is also my choice—I can choose to be nice to my body and get a massage, take aspirin, fall asleep, or go to the acupuncturist. But it's my choice how I respond. All of these "solutions" are just tools that I'm choosing to use. And here is the cool part ... the feeling of the headache isn't me. The headache is just something I'm experiencing and is showing me where I'm not in coherence ... where my thoughts and feelings aren't lined up.

I also get to choose if I keep the pain or not. I can choose to play with it or to put it somewhere else. Sometimes, I've even taken a headache and thrown it into another dimension where it's more useful. Amazingly, it worked. It was as easy as imagining that I was grabbing the pain and literally throwing it a couple of dimensions over. In my head, I'm imagining the *blub, blub, blub* as the pain wiggles through invisible barriers between dimensions. The important thing is to play with it and allow something different. (For more about images like this, take a look at Matrix Energetics.)

But what about the consistent stuff? It's still you having an experience. Just knowing that you can observe it lessens the pain some. Ask yourself, "Is this me or is this something I'm experiencing?"

It seems like a lot of responsibility to think that you are choosing to experience pain. On a logical level, most people wouldn't want to experience pain; however, the pain allows for communication between the conscious mind and the subconscious mind. Our subconscious mind, which we don't control, doesn't think or follow rules of logic. It just keeps repeating memorized patterns of behavior and process. And it can only communicate with the conscious in one of two ways: feelings (body sensations) or symbols (like dreams).

Pain is a very powerful body sensation to get the attention of the conscious mind. Imagine if you broke a bone in your foot but had no pain, continued to walk on it, and caused further damage! However, pain or other body sensations function more like an "idiot light" in a car rather than a gauge or computer read out. It lets you know something is not congruent (your thoughts and feelings don't match up), but can't necessarily tell you specifically what it is.

Start with a Desire and Move to the Feeling of Knowing.

All in all, it's about knowing what it is you desire. People often confuse "want" and "desire." "Want" implies lack. "Desire" implies hope and intention. The vibrations of the words are different. "Lack" feels heavy, whereas "hope and intention" feel light.

Some people think *want* is a bad word and have made up a rule that says *we should be happy with whatever we have.* But if someone believes these rules, then they are blocking improvement in their life. They'll never strive for something different or better. They might as well be a blob. Nothing will change ... unless they desire for something to be different. This desire to have something better—to be better—pushes humanity forward. If it wasn't there, we'd still be living in the Stone Age, and something as simple as the wheel would never have been invented. It's when you get stuck in the wanting feeling and never feel that you have whatever it is you want that life seems to stall out.

When you move from the wanting to the sense of knowing that you already have it, you are on your way. It's just a matter of time (filled with positive action) until you have it. You can even make up a rule that *as soon as I think it, it's already done.* Then all you have to do is fill your time with the positive actions that will support your desire. Be sure to pay attention to the clues the Universe lays at your feet. They are showing you the right way to achieve what you know is already done, but not quite in your hands yet. But it will be shortly.

This happened when I decided to be a teacher. I was coaching girls' gymnastics at my high school after I graduated college while I was trying to figure out what to do with my life. The head coach said he couldn't pay me unless I had a teaching certificate. Okay. I figured this would be easy. I already had a double major in business, and *teaching was easy.* (After all, I'd been coaching since I was about 14, and I liked to teach. And I never really liked business school anyway.)

I set about finding a graduate school near my home that I didn't have to write a thesis for, which considering I'm a writer is funny. After failing the entrance exam, they welcomed me in anyway. (Notice I already saw myself at a very good teacher's college, and the school agreed. What did it matter if I'm terrible at "this is to that" type of tests?) I asked which classes I had to take to get my certificate and took those, out of order, and with a heavier course load then they wanted me to no less. With that, I got my teaching certification within nine months.

I knew I was going to get a teaching job even though everyone else said there weren't any. I sent my resume to every school district in the county north of me and in the northern and western parts of my county. Then I called every district every week for two months. I found lots of jobs, many of which I wasn't qualified for, but passed on the leads to the job office at the college. Long story short, I found a job as a full-time substitute, and they hired me as a teacher the next year. I went on to finish my master's degree, taught school, and never happened to go back to my high school to coach. But the sign was to get my teaching certification.

But it started with a desire. The desire was to find what I really liked to do. As I followed the signs in front of me, I just knew . . . I had the feeling of knowing that I'd have it. Then I put in the positive actions to get there.

You Can Change Your Reality

Just because reality shows up one way for you doesn't mean it will always, or even that it has to show up that way again. If I'd let the "reality" of my failed entrance exam determine my reality, I might have missed out on the opportunity to be a teacher. However, I knew I'd be a teacher. Beyond that, I let the Universe sort it all out for me. I just followed the signs.

Because of the knowing, I didn't see the failed exam as a sign. In fact, I learned that if a student fails, it's not the end of the world. Learn from it and move forward. Don't get stuck in the failure. (Good advice for when you or your teens make mistakes.)

You don't have to fail to change your reality. You can just choose something different. For example, I often ask the angels for help to change my reality. One time I was driving to downtown Chicago from the northern suburbs at five o'clock on a Friday afternoon. It's possible for this trip to take two hours because of rush hour, which by the way is only a reality for those who think it is. However, I had a dinner date with a friend at 5:45 and had gotten off to a late start. Luckily, I'd just learned about Archangel Merlin from Belinda Womack (the angel communicator). He's in charge of time and helps with traffic, among other things. So, I sent up a prayer asking Merlin to have me arrive at the restaurant at 5:45. I then let it go, knowing that he would make it happen. And he did. I pulled up at the valet in front of the restaurant at exactly 5:45.

I didn't keep asking. I didn't fret about it. I had the feeling that *whatever happened would be to my benefit.* (Did you notice the rule?) I didn't keep checking the time and cursing the drivers around me for being in my way. All I did was enjoy the ride and marvel at how easy it was. Although, I did throw in a few thanks while I was driving.

So, let's go over what happened here. I asked Archangel Merlin for what I desired. I let it go. And I had a sense of knowing that it was being taken care of, and I didn't need to keep asking him. I didn't have to figure out how Merlin was going to do it. I expected Merlin to come through for me and for me to arrive on time. And as I pulled up in front of the restaurant at 5:45, I thanked him (big time).

Remember to identify exactly what you desire, see it as if it's already done, get the knowing feeling, and then be grateful for having it. If you view it in this way, you can change your reality. Rewrite your life within yourself to reflect the way you desire your reality to be just like I did by seeing myself in front of the restaurant at the correct time.

Once you've identified your desire, take the time to decide what it will look like—so that when it does happen, you can recognize it. I could have said I expected to arrive downtown at 5:45, but I could have still been late, as downtown Chicago is very big and I could have still been miles away from the location of the restaurant. Or I could have asked for traffic to flow quickly; but again, that wouldn't assure me that I'd get to the restaurant on time. Or I could have asked for a parking place on the street ... although I never expect these. However my daughter, Bethany, does, and she frequently gets them. (She has the rule that *everything always works out for her*.)

But you get the idea. Take the time to determine exactly what you expect to happen. Then expect it.

Allowing Possibilities Gets You to the Knowing

Too often people have a thought or feeling and then get stuck with it. It's as if they poured glue over the idea and it can never shift. However, in reality, thoughts and feelings are changeable ... if we allow the possibility for something different.

The simplest way to allow for a new possibility is to ask yourself, **"If it was possible, could I allow ... ?"** It's that easy. This simple question opens the mind and allows something different to come in; and very often, this is something unexpected. A great way to play with this is to ask the question repeatedly. Be sure to say a resounding "YES!" after each question. This tells the Universe that you can allow for the possibility. At some point in the exercise, it will feel done. Trust the feeling. Pay attention to what shows up in your life. You will know that you need to do this exercise more if what is showing up isn't what you desire. Just keep reordering. (Remember the restaurant?)

Let's look at an example of how to get unstuck in our thinking. (The same question can be used for feelings.) I had a client who was cheated in a business deal. He'd had a rule that *he was always taken advantage of instead of loved for who he is.* He was hurt; and in his hurt, he was ranting and raving about everything he would do. Needless to say, he was stuck in the negative thinking. But he was smart enough to know that if he stayed there, something better would be kept from him until he changed his thoughts and feelings. So, we started out with me asking:

"If it was possible, could you allow yourself to feel as bad as you do in this moment?"

He responded, "YES!" (He was giving himself permission to feel what he already felt.)

"If it was possible, could you allow that things will get better?"

He responded, "Yes." (Even though it was a weak yes, it was still a yes.)

"If it was possible, could you allow that even though you don't know how, something better will come from this?"

"Yes." (This one was a little bit stronger.)

"If it was possible, could you allow that in some way, this is all perfect?"

"Yes." (He'd been listening to me long enough to know that *things have a way of working out.*)

"If it was possible, could you allow that an even better opportunity will come around?"

"Yes." (It was getting a little stronger.)

"If it was possible, could you allow that you don't have to know what the opportunity is at this moment?"

"Yes." (Now we were in the flow.)

"If it was possible, could you allow that the opportunity will come to you?"

"Yes."

"If it was possible, could you allow that you can forgive yourself for the vibration you were feeling that 'seemed to cause' this experience?"

"Yes."

"If it was possible, could you allow your feelings to change?"

"Yes."

"If it was possible, could you allow that the people who participated in this experience will 'get theirs' and karma will take care of them?"

"Yes."

"If it was possible, could you allow the feeling of something different?"

"Yes."

"If it was possible, could you allow new ideas to come to you that are even better?"

"Yes."

"If it was possible, could you allow the situation to work out in your favor?"

"Yes."

"If it was possible, could you allow the situation to resolve without you having to do anything?"

"Yes."

"If it was possible, could you allow ..." You get the idea.

(I like this step-by-step approach. Some consciousness programs or energy transformation systems lump it all together and ask if you could allow infinite possibilities. This can work too. The idea is to stay open to the possibility of something different and better.)

Notice I stayed on the path of where he wanted to go (things working out), not the path that he was already on (being cheated). The more energy we put into things working out, the more his blood pressure lowered, and he started to feel good again. We finished up with the hand-balancing exercise to neutralize some of the remaining feelings around his rule and how it showed up in his life. We could have started there, but his feelings were so intense that it was easier to get into shifting the energy by asking questions.

As it turned out, an even better opportunity did present itself the next night, and constructive ideas about how to deal with the "cheaters" began flowing. All in all, he feels very good about the ending, even if he didn't like how it started.

It's Done

To get to the knowing feeling even faster, adopt the rule: *It's done as soon as I think of it.* Be sure to clear the feelings that come up around this new rule. I guarantee you there will be feelings.

When Dr. Jahner told me this book was already written, I was skeptical. I thought I was working very hard to bring this book into physical form. However, when someone asked me to write a newsletter article for her publication, I instinctively said, "It's done" as soon as we discussed what the parameters of the article were. Then by the time I got home, the article was written in my head, and I sat down at the computer to type it out. For something that I had a month to complete, I was literally done with it in less than a day. I finally understood what Dr. Jahner meant. I applied it to this book, and the unwritten part of it flowed out of me.

CHAPTER 18
Consciousness Concept Review

. . . .

Reality/Change/Knowing/It's Done

▶ Be a true observer in your own life.

▶ Is the experience me, or is it just something I'm
  experiencing?

▶ Pain is a very powerful body sensation to get the
  attention of the conscious mind.

▶ People often confuse "want" and "desire." "Want"
  implies lack. "Desire" implies hope and intention.

▶ You don't have to fail to change your reality. You can
  choose something different.

▶ Ask, "If it was possible, could I allow _____?"

▶ It's done as soon as I think of it.

. . . .

Done Exercise

How to do it:

1. When you choose to do something, adopt the rule: It's done as soon as I think of it.
2. Then say: "Done."
3. The Universe will lay out the steps for you to accomplish it; all you have to do is take the positive actions to bring it into your physical reality.

REM:

Repetition: The more you use this rule, the easier things are to accomplish.

Emotion: Saying it with a knowing that it's already done (in theory). It just has to get done in the timing we call reality.

Motion: Saying it out loud will give it more emphasis and power.

Purpose:

This makes everything easier. You're telling the Universe what you expect.

Weird Visuals (This is my favorite.)

How to do it:

1. Ask yourself, "If I were to see something, what might it be?"
2. Trust whatever shows up.
3. Keep asking questions. Watch what shows up.
   a. What is above/below, inside/outside/on, in front of/behind whatever you initially saw?
   b. What color is it?
   c. What is it doing?
   d. Who else is there and what are they doing?
   e. What does it want to say to me?
   f. Where does it want to go?
4. Look at everything as interesting and important only in the fact that it leads you to the next question. Each piece is not supposed to make sense by itself. Trust your intuition. In the end, you'll know what the whole thing is about.

REM:

Repetition: The more you do weird visuals, the easier they become. But one visual (with many questions) is sufficient to answer a question or move the energy in that moment.

Emotion: Feelings will pop up. View each as "that's interesting." Don't get invested in one feeling being the "right one."

Motion: I move my eyes and head as if I'm actually looking at a picture. Or you can paint the picture by moving your hands in the air, moving the colors and images around.

Purpose:

Weird visuals help to reveal things in your subconscious mind and bring them out into the open.

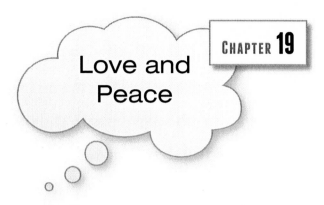

Love and Peace

The Heart of all Other Rules

I've been experimenting with an idea, and I like it. It actually changes how I feel in the moment. It slows me down and allows me to take a breath, feel better, and be more loving. As often happens, I use drive time as a time to think things through. And as I contemplated this particular idea, I could see the changes happening before me. Things became clearer. I became more patient with the other drivers. (Actually, I became more patient with myself.) I let the other drivers go first at the stop sign. I let the pedestrians cross the street without me getting impatient. I actually sat back and enjoyed giving them a chance to go first.

And all I did was ask myself three questions. But these questions were reminders to me about love. (The questions are on page 157 if you can't wait.)

According to Dr. Jahner (who was quoting Jesus), there are two basic principles. The first principle is to *love God*. The second is to *love others as you do yourself.* All the other rules and laws fall under these two principles. The idea is to get to the point where we don't need any rules (other than these two principles).

As Dr. Jahner and I continued to talk, I began to understand what this was about. He compared each of us to a facet of a diamond. Each facet is complete in that it is a beautiful facet. But the purpose of all the facets is to help the entire diamond sparkle. Together all the facets form the diamond. The entire diamond is God. We are each a facet of God. We need each other to form the whole.

(In full disclosure, I'm Jewish; and while I think Jesus was a great teacher and rabbi, Jesus was just quicker on the uptake than the rest of us about God's love. And even if you believe he never truly existed, the ideas attributed to him are good.)

Rules have been made up to help us achieve these two principles. However, once we understand why the rules are there, we don't need them any more. The clue is not to focus on the rules. Focus on the underlying purpose. Unfortunately, people think the rules become more important than the purpose behind the rules. Whereas the rules are just guidelines to help us get back to love ... loving God, ourselves, and others.

Let's take a moment and look at the two principles. First, love God. This sounded easy, but I could feel more acceptance with the idea when I added ... "as God loves me." It wasn't just me "putting out" the effort. Maybe God's love was implied. If God loves and is love and God created everything, then everything was created out of love. Wait a minute. Everything is made of love? Imagine if each cell of everything was actually love. Would that change how you feel about yourself? Others? Things? It's just a thought. But I start from where I'm at, so here I am..."Love God as God loves me."

Moving on. The second principle deals with your relationship with yourself and others. Love others as you do yourself. This automatically implies that you love yourself. So loving yourself has to come first, then you can love others (people, animals, etc.). If we love ourselves and then treat other people the way we treat ourselves, this might cause us to step back and notice how we are treating ourselves. Are you really loving yourself if you are abusing your body? Are you loving yourself if you talk bad about yourself? Are you loving yourself if you continuously don't get enough sleep? Are you loving yourself if you aren't listening to the messages your body is giving you? Take a moment and ask yourself if you are being loving to yourself in this moment.

Very often, what we get mad at in others is actually something that we don't like about ourselves. But since the other person is just a reflection of us, we get mad at them instead of looking within and loving ourselves more.

One of my son's past girlfriends decided that she didn't trust him because he could look and see that other girls/women were beautiful. (We're talking a three second glance, not an all-out stare.) She bullied him about this until he drew a line and said, "No more. This isn't what I desire in a relationship."

In short, she sabotaged a loving relationship because of her jealousy. In truth, her own self esteem wasn't strong (which means that her loving herself was difficult), so she got mad at my son when he couldn't love her by never noticing that anyone else is beautiful. When in fact, he saw her beauty inside and out regardless of whatever else was out there. *She* was the one who couldn't see her own beauty and own it.

This even leads to the idea that one of the most important things we can teach our children is to love themselves and treat themselves kindly. I'm not talking about the ego-inflating type of love, but the respect, acceptance, and kindness kind of love. Imagine how nice the world would be if we all loved ourselves and treated ourselves with respect and kindness. This would ooze out; and since the world is a mirror, and what we are feeling inside would be reflected in what we attract to us, if we are feeling love, respect, and kindness, then that is what we would be getting back ... experiences of love, respect, and kindness. And just imagine how peaceful the world could be if we each loved ourselves and accepted that others could love themselves.

However much you love yourself is how much you can love others. Some people think it's the other way around and move toward loving themselves by loving others. For example, we all feel better when we take the time to help someone else. But underneath it, you have to love yourself enough to desire to help others. However much you love yourself is how much you will be able to love others. This leads to how you treat yourself and how you treat others.

Feelings are our guiding light. The goal is to live in the love feeling and then use the other feelings that come up as indicators that something is different from love. We can then choose what to do with the feeling and whatever is causing it. However, here's a hint ... the more you are in the love feelings, the easier your life is, and the less things bother you. (Instead of love, you can measure against peace, lightness, expansiveness, joy, etc. if you like.)

So, what prevents us from setting the intention to just live in the love feeling all the time? Habit. We aren't used to it. Somewhere along the way, we fell off the wagon of love, and we have spent the rest of our lives trying to find that feeling again. Unfortunately, many of us are looking outside ourselves in relationships, things, etc. in an attempt to find the love. What we don't realize is that the feeling of love is within us, and get this ... the origin of love is also within us. It's our choice if we want to feel it or not.

Everything put together ... The Universe is made out of love. When we bring ourselves in harmony with love, we will have success in life.

So, what are the three questions?

- ▶ Am I being loving toward God?
- ▶ Am I being loving toward myself?
- ▶ Am I being loving toward others?

Think about these for a minute. The answers are either yes or no. If the answer is yes, then you will feel great, and life will be successful. However, if the answer is no (even a tiny bit), then you have an opportunity to be, feel, and do something different so that you can get to a yes answer.

Or you can ask, "Could I allow more loving?" This is simple. It doesn't restrict the flow of loving to or from you or others. All you are doing is allowing more loving into your reality. It's not as if you will answer, "No. I'm full up on loving and can't add another drop." Just bringing your attention to the love feeling allows more to flow to and from you.

What if life were that simple? What if *the only rule we need is to love*?

But that leads to the question, "What is love?"

For me, love is acceptance and peace within myself, whether it is for myself or someone or something else. But is that your definition?

While talking about love with my father, he asked for the definition of love because he didn't know what it meant. This got me thinking. What if everyone else has a different definition of love? What if your definition isn't the same as mine?

I've been asking my family and friends, and it seems as if everyone has a little different definition. So, I'd like to explore this further. Please take a moment and e-mail me your definition of love. The next book I'm planning is "What is Love?" I'd love to include your definition. Sending me your answer is your permission to be included in the book. Please let me know if you'd like your name in the book or if you'd like another identifier such as, Love Bug. Send your definition of love to: judith_joy@aol.com.

CHAPTER 19
Consciousness Concept Review

Love and Peace

▶ However much you love yourself is how much you can love others.

▶ Ask yourself:

> Am I being loving toward God?
> Am I being loving toward myself?
> Am I being loving toward others?
> Could I allow more loving?

Snuggle Energy Exercise

How to do it:

1. Imagine snuggling with a happy baby.
2. Imagine the baby looking at you with trust and love.
3. Feel your heart open up with love for the baby.
4. Increase this feeling of love until it fills you and spills out of you.

REM:

Repetition: The goal is to live in this snuggle energy all the time; so the more you do it, the more you will feel it.

Emotion: Love.

Motion: Imagine actually holding a cuddly, cooing baby. You can even hold your arms as if you are holding the baby and rocking it.

Purpose:

Snuggle energy helps to build the feeling of love within you.

Expand from the Heart Exercise

How to do it:

1. Imagine and feel the love in your heart.
2. Slowly imagine the energy of this emotion getting bigger and bigger.
3. Expand the energy as far as it can go. Be sure to imagine the energy expanding in all directions: front, back, right, left, up, and down.
4. Imagine the energy rippling out in waves in inches, feet, miles, states, countries, the entire world, and beyond.
5. After expanding all the way beyond the stars, bring the energy back into your heart.
6. In short: Be still. Breathe into your heart. Connect with the God within you.

REM:

Repetition: Do the complete exercise three or more times.

Emotion: The more you can imagine the feeling of gathering and moving the energy, the better the exercise will be. You will eventually be able to feel instead of just imagine.

Motion: This can be done with just imagination. However, including movements helps to make it more real and thus more powerful.

Purpose:

This exercise expands the energy in your heart, which is your source of power. It also helps feelings dissipate and dissolve, which in turn brings your desires closer to manifestation. This allows you to step into your power and be a better you.

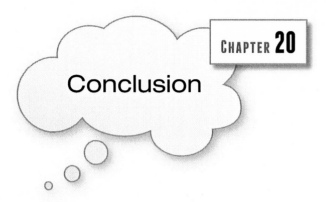

CHAPTER 20

Conclusion

The Process All Put Together

When you first picked up this book, you possibly had the assumption that it would help you in some way with your teenager. And on some level, I'll bet you want your teen to change so you can be happy. But you can't change someone else—you can only change yourself. You are your teen's greatest teacher. Whether you like it or not, *you* are the one showing your teen the way things can be. It's your choice what type of role model you decide to be.

You get to create your own reality in this Universe. How you view what happens to you is up to you. You get to decide what you desire, what your intention is, how it will feel, and how you will recognize it when it shows up. Then all you have to do is know that it's yours as you step out of the way to allow the possibilities to flow to you.

Even when things don't go your way, you get to choose how you respond. Look for how they can work for you. Respond to everything with, "GREAT! I wonder how this will benefit me? How can it get better than that?" Take the time to look for the good and then allow more good to flow your way.

Let's end with a visualization to bring it all together ...

Begin by walking into the elevator in your mind. Watch as the doors close. Do you feel the silence as you leave behind the chatter in your mind? What if there was joy in this silence?

Ride the elevator down to your heart level and watch as the doors open. Do you feel the love that is there? Allow the feelings of peace, acceptance, and love to flow through you and around you. Feel your heart field expand. As it does, the feelings become stronger and stronger. There is so much love that you can't help but let it spill out of you. And what if you felt even more love? Could you allow yourself the possibility of feeling even more love?

Expand the love energy and power of your heart. Fill your body with the energy. Expand it outward. Go further and further until your energy is in the entire galaxy reaching past the stars.

Look around the heart field. What do you see? Do you see your desire? Do you see your intention? Where is it? What does it look like? What feeling does it have? What feeling is this desire giving you? How many ways can it be even better? What color is your desire? Is there anything near it? Is it attached to something else? What is this? What does it have to say to you?

Can you see how happy your desire is to finally be seen by you? Can you allow yourself to take delight in having it? Can you allow it to feel even better? Imagine it coming to you and sharing its love.

Stay in the questioning mode as you discover your desires and feelings by listening for the answers from your inner self—your spirit communicating with you. Listen to the truth within you. Listen to your intuition. Use your truth barometer.

Just in case there are any thoughts and feelings popping up (as we know they will), be sure to balance and neutralize them. This will allow you to be clear and open to receiving your true desire. Step into the possibility thinking. If it were possible for this desire to come to you, could you allow it? Do you feel something in your body? Could you allow this feeling to neutralize, melt, disappear, leave, or in some other way change? Could you allow them to go? You can try hand balancing to help the energy to neutralize. (Repeat the possibility questions and allow the energy to move.)

Immediately, the Universe will be throwing signs (answers to your questions) in your path. Stay on the lookout for them. Then follow these signs to the positive actions that will help you achieve your intentions.

When your true desire is ready, (when the timing is best, not necessarily when you think it will be), it will show up in your life ... possibly in some way you didn't expect. Stay open to the possibilities of your true feelings showing up over and over in many different forms.

This is the magic of the Universe. You have asked; it has responded. If you don't like what shows up, ask for something else ... whatever it is that you really, truly desire and your feelings resonate with. Then when it shows up, receive it with open arms and give thanks.

The closer you are to love, peace, and acceptance, the easier life becomes ... and the happier you are. And along the way, your teen may decide to emulate you ... especially if you dialogue with your teen about the changes you are experiencing and the positive effects that are showing up in your life. After all, you are the example. You are the love.

Internal Workout Space

This section has additional exercises that will help you focus on the possibilities and feelings you desire while increasing your imagination and intuition. They will help you set your intentions into motion. It doesn't matter what order you try them in. The important thing is to do something and reach for a better feeling.

I've tried to use exercises that span all the consciousness programs and energy transformation systems. As with all the exercises in this book, if I've included an exercise that is specific to only one program, I've noted it. For example, in the first exercise (Moment to Moment Joy Exercise), note that the how to do it is general. How it shows up (the actual visual) is how a specific consciousness program or energy transformation system may use it.

Moment To Moment Joy Exercise

How to do it:

1. Stand in an open space.
2. Ask your body, "What will make me joyful in this moment?"
3. Listen for the answer.
4. Take a step.
5. Repeat steps 2–4.
6. By the end of the exercise, you will have a collection of things that will increase your joy and happiness. Do one or more of them.

REM:

Repetition: The more steps you take (they don't have to be in a straight line), the more ways you have uncovered to bring joy into your life.

Emotion: The more joy you uncover, the better you feel.

Motion: This can be done sitting; but the more motion you put into it, the more likely you are to stay on task and think of more possibilities.

Purpose:

This exercise helps you stay in the moment, asks your body what it desires, and helps you feel better.

Gratitude Statements Exercise

How to do it:

1. Say, "I'm grateful for _____."
2. Find something else you are grateful for.
3. Find something else you are grateful for.
4. If you are dealing with a seemingly negative situation, you can begin with, "Even though _____, I'm grateful for it because _____."

REM:

Repetition: Repeat often. The more you do it, the more things you will see to be grateful for.

Emotion: You will feel better and better.

Motion: Saying gratitude statements is effective. Writing them down is more powerful.

Purpose:

Gratitude statements help raise your vibration; and the more you say them, the more good you will find, and the better you will feel.

What is Your Part?

How to do it:

1. When something happens to you (such as your child yells at you), ask yourself, "What is my part in this?"
2. Be open to the idea that you have played some part (even if it's how you behaved in the past) in why things are as they are in this moment.
3. All you have to do is acknowledge your part.

REM:

Repetition: Do it all the time—even for simple things like traffic.

Emotion: Especially do this exercise when your feelings are heightened.

Motion: I like to pretend I have a card file or rolodex in front of me. I flip through the "cards" until one seems to be it. It's not important that I "read" every card. It's only important that I stay with it until I find the one that feels right.

Purpose:

If you do this every time a situation arises, you will begin to take personal responsibility for what shows up in your life. You will be able to then decide if you want to behave or feel the same. Then you can make a choice to do something different.

Bubble Up Exercise

How to do it:
1. Feel a feeling in your body.
2. Imagine you are blowing bubbles out of your body.
3. Watch as each bubble floats away or pops. This is the energy of the feeling leaving your body.

REM:
Repetition: Stay with this exercise until there aren't any more bubbles to let go of.

Emotion: This exercise is used with any emotion and allows the emotion to dissipate.

Motion: Imagine the feeling moving out of your body in the form of bubbles.

Purpose:
Moving the energy of the feeling through your body and allowing it to leave helps you let go of the feeling and allows for something better to come in.

Laughter

How to do it:

1. This can be done individually, but it's better with a group. Laugh.
2. Try giggles, belly laughs, and any other type of laughing you can think of.

REM:

Repetition: The more you do, the better you feel. Start with a minimum of one minute.

Emotion: Laughing shifts your mood to something better.

Motion: Stand up and get your whole body into the laughter.

Purpose:

Laughter releases pent-up energy and helps you feel better. Your vibration will actually increase just from laughter.

Deep Breathing

How to do it:

1. Slowly take a deep breath until you fill your entire lungs (inhale as if the bottom of your lungs were located in your bellybutton).
2. Slowly exhale.
3. Some techniques say hold your breath between the inhale and exhale. Other techniques say to exhale and then hold your breath. The important thing is to slow down your breathing and inhale oxygen.
4. You can imagine filling your body (down to your toes and up to your head) with air. You can even imagine that the air is a color and the color is moving through your body.

REM:

Repetition: One is good. More is better. Try doing deep breathing for 15 minutes a day.

Emotion: Deep breathing allows your feelings to calm down.

Motion: Your whole body can be involved with the breathing. This can be done while sitting, laying, and walking... although if you are actually moving, the breathing may be from the exertion. You are still getting oxygen, but it's a little bit different.

Purpose:

Deep breathing moves stuck energy and helps you feel calmer. It also helps you to listen to the silence and increases your intuition.

Letting Go

How to do it:
1. Feel the feeling.
2. Put it somewhere outside of yourself.
3. Watch as it leaves.
4. There are many visual ways to accomplish this.
   a. **Cosmic toilet** – Imagine a giant toilet. Put anything you don't want (including feelings) into the toilet. Flush and watch as it swirls and leaves in the purple water of transformation. (Spiritual College of Evolution)
   b. **Cartoon Surgery** – Imagine a surgeon (I like to imagine a cartoon figure) who is pulling out whatever you need or desire. The items the cartoon surgeon is pulling out don't even have to make sense such as old dressers, rusty screwdrivers, and doggie kibbles. They are symbolic and represent something, but you don't have to know what. (Matrix Energetics)
   c. **Transformation Train** – Put whatever you don't want on a train and watch as it leaves. (Spiritual College of Evolution)

REM:
Repetition: Look within you for more things related to what you are letting go of.

Emotion: Have a knowing feeling that you are moving the energy. Feel within your body as it leaves.

Motion: Hand movements always help.

Purpose:
This exercise helps you get rid of all aspects of something. It helps you let go.

Colors

How to do it:

1. Different colors have different properties.
2. If you look at the different consciousness programs or energy transformation systems, they will have lists of the colors and their properties. I'm including three colors I use a lot.
   a. **White** – Purity. Imagine taking a shower of white light or walking through white light, or the white light is within you burning away whatever is "impure," thus leaving purity.
   b. **Purple** – Transformation. Wash something with purple. Swim in purple water. Add purple to a feeling. Purple is used to transform something, allows change, and allows something to be different.
   c. **Cobalt Blue** – Set a boundary. Use a blue curtain in a doorway to keep others out (such as small children who are learning to sleep in their own beds). Use blue surrounding your car to protect it and you as you drive. Use blue to tell the Universe that you don't want to talk with a person. (I used this when a married man was pursuing me. I put up a blue wall. He stopped calling. Months later, he called again. I figured the blue wall fell down, and so I just put it up in my mind again.)

REM:

Repetition: One time is good.

Emotion: Have a knowing feeling that it works.

Motion: No motion is needed, but I have imagined a wall of white and actually walked through "it."

Purpose:

To allow change and something better to come in.

Psychic E-Mail

How to do it:
1. Determine what it is you truly desire for someone to hear.
2. Put it in language that is positive. (Drop the word "not.")
3. Give the message to your spiritual self.
4. Ask your spiritual self to talk with the spiritual self of the other person to give him your message.

REM:
Repetition: One message is sufficient.

Emotion: Whatever feeling you are feeling as you compose the message will be delivered to the other person. Make sure the feeling is one you intend to share.

Motion: Imagine the message going inside you, up above you, shooting through the air like e-mail, and then down into the other person.

Purpose:
This is a good way to tell the Universe what you desire so that the Universe can bring the message to the other person. (This actually works, even though it sounds weird.)

Connection Exercise

How to do it:

1. Decide what it is you truly hope for or desire.
2. Focus on the feeling behind this.
3. Point to where it is located. It doesn't matter if it's on or in you or off of you in space somewhere.
4. Connect that point to you by focusing on the connection. This can be seen as "pulling" the desired feeling into you.
5. There are many visual ways to do this exercise.
   a. **Windows** – Picture a wall of windows. The desired feeling is in one of the windows. (Matrix Energetics)
   b. **Outside Picture** – Look out of an imaginary window or outside of your body. See the desired feeling. Connect what you see to your body.
   c. **Library** – Picture a library filled with books. The desired feeling is in one or more of the books. Take the book from the shelf and "read it." This can also be used to take out the rules and feelings that no longer work for you. Just empty the shelves of the books you no longer need. Imagine sending them out into the world where they will be more useful. (College of Spiritual Evolution)
   d. **Chemistry Set** – Picture a chemistry set with many vials of "feelings." Combine the feelings you desire into a beaker and mix together. Then decide what to do with the new combination … use it as a cream on yourself, drink it, pour it over your head, etc.
   e. **Recipe** – Picture a pastry or even a drink. Each of the ingredients is a feeling that you are asking to be in

your reality. Picture yourself adding these feelings to the pastry or drink. Prepare it and then eat/drink it.

f. **Paint a picture** – This can be done in the magical, imaginary realm, or you can actually paint what you desire.

REM:

Repetition: The more you do these exercises/visualizations, the easier they become. Only one time is needed; but since we run on memorized patterns, more times can certainly be done.

Emotion: Being neutral and open allows the best possibilities to come to you. By allowing the feeling instead of the exact item, you are opening the doors to something even better.

Motion: I like to use physical motion with this one. It looks as if I'm just waving my hands around, but I'm actually pointing to the feeling and bringing it into my heart. If I'm mixing something, I actually use my hands as if I'm "really" mixing everything.

Purpose:

You are outlining and filling in the details of what you expect to show up in your life. You are placing the order and letting the Universe bring it to you. In short, this exercise helps you focus on what you do desire instead of what you don't.

Appendix: B

Glossary

Awareness: Being aware. Having knowledge. Consciousness.

Balance: The act of neutralizing. Taking the emotional charge off of the feelings.

Coherence: When things work together.

Conditioned You: Who you are after you have accepted the rules, thoughts, beliefs, etc. of others.

Consciousness: The full awareness of all that is.

Conscious Mind: The part of your mind that is aware of all the possibilities.

Emotion: A sensation is a feeling in the body. The emotion is the label used to describe that sensation.

Energy: The energetic force that allows for things to shift and change.

Feeling: The sensation of an emotion. How it actually feels in your body. When feelings are stuck, they create pain.

Gut Check: Check in with your body to find what is truth for you and what isn't.

Hand Balancing: The act of balancing two thoughts, emotions, etc. in the hands with the aim of neutralizing the emotional charge of each.

Higher Self: The intelligent being that is you.

Morphic Field: The energy state surrounding a belief or practice believed to be true by many people.

Neutral: No emotional charge.

Subconscious Mind: The part of the mind that is not aware in the moment of the possibilities.

Pain: A signal to the body that something is out of coherence. Something is out of balance and the energy is stuck.

Possibility Thinking: Asking questions to allow for new possibilities.

Rules: Beliefs we tell ourselves.

Spirit: The essence of who you are.

Truth Barometer: The gut check. What feels true is light and expansive. What feels false is heavy, dark, or constrictive. Different programs have different methods for expressing this.

Unconditioned You: The person you were born as without the conditioning of others.

Universe: All that is. Can also be referred to as God, Light, Spirit, etc. The Universe has a force or energy to allow all the possibilities to come to you.

Vibration: Tiny movements that are extremely fast. Everything vibrates and attracts or repels based on this harmonic signal.

Appendix: C

Bibliography

Consciousness Programs & Energy Transformation Systems

Abraham-Hicks, Esther & Jerry Hicks, www.abraham-hicks.com
  Channeled information. Law of Attraction.

Access Consciousness, Gary Douglas and Dr. Dain Heer, www.access consciousness.com
  Lots of great questions. Mind expanding. Hands-on component.

Anamika, www.anamika.com
  Medical intuitive. Individual and group sessions about expanding your consciousness.

College of Spiritual Evolution, Belinda Womack, www.belindawom ack.com (While her college has closed, Belinda continues to teach and coach.)
  Informative. Loving. Mind expanding.

Happiness Project and Success Intelligence, Robert Holden, PhD, http://www.happiness.co.uk
  Robert is pure love. Very informative and lots of exercises.

Healing Light Church, Rosalyn Bruyere, www.rosalynlbruyere.org
  I learned to feel energy with this. The program has grown a lot since I took the classes with a student of Rosalyn's.

IBMS, Instinct Based Medicine System, Dr. Leonard Coldwell, www.instinctbasedmedicine.com

Great audios. Work with an IBMS coach. Effective. Get ready for some hard hitting. Hands-on component.

Matrix Energetics, Dr. Richard Bartlett, www.matrixenergetics.com
My favorite. Fun. Creative. Hands-on or long distance. He explains the science behind energy healing.

Neurometabolic Reintegration, Dr. Ron Jahner, www.intentional network.com, www.gordinmedical.com
Dr. Jahner, my mentor, is insightful, patient, and very talented. He can feel and shift the energy all while teaching. He is a wonderful conduit for healing.

Release Technique, Lester Levinson & Larry Crane, www.release technique.com
Involves digging deep. Good for an organized, structured approach.

Spring Forest Qigong, Chunyi Lin, www.springforestqigong.com
I learned to feel energy with this. The program has grown a lot since I took the classes.

Books & Magazines

Allen, James, *As A Man Thinketh* (New York: Barnes & Noble Books, 2002)

Angel, Janet, *All That You Are* (1st Books Library, 2001)

Bartlett, Richard, DC, ND, *Matrix Energetics* (New York: Atria Books, Simon & Schuster, 2007)

Bartlett, Richard, DC, ND, *The Physics of Miracles* (New York: Atria Books, Simon & Schuster, 2009)

Braden, Gregg, *Spontaneous Healing of Belief* (California: Hay House, Inc., 2008)

Braden, Gregg, *The Divine Matrix* (California: Hay House, Inc., 2007)

Bristol, Claude M. *The Magic of Believing* (New York: A Fireside Book, Simon & Schuster, 1985)

Brodie, Richard, *Virus of the Mind* (California: Hay House, Inc., 1996)

Bruyere, Rosalyn L., *Wheels of Light* (New York: Fireside, Simon & Schuster, 1989, 1991, 1994)

Buffett, Peter, *Life is What You Make It* (New York: Harmony Books, Crown Publishing Group, 2010)

Coldwell, Leonard NMD, DNM, Ph.D., LCHC, CNHP, DIP.PHC, *The Only Answer to Cancer* (21 C Publishers, 2011)

Coldwell, Leonard, NMD, DNM, Ph.D., LCHC, CNHP, DIP.PHC, *The Only Answer to Stress, Anxiety & Depression* (21 C Publishers, 2010)

Coldwell, Leonard, NMD, DNM, Ph.D., LCHC, CNHP, DIP.PHC, The Only Answer to Success (21 C Publishers, 2010)

Coldwell, Leonard, NMD, DNM, Ph.D., LCHC, CNHP, DIP.PHC, The Only Answer to Surviving Your Illness and Your Doctor (21 C Publishers, 2011)

Collins, Dianne, *Do You Quantum Think?* (New York, SelectBooks, Inc. 2011)

Crane, Lawrence, *Love Yourself and Let the Other Person Have it Your Way* (California: Release Technique, LP, 2009)

Crane, Lawrence, *The Abundance Book* (California: Lawrence Crane Enterprises, Inc., 1998)

Csikszentmihalyi, Mihaly, *Flow* (New York: Harper Perennial, Harper Collins Publishers, 1990)

Douglas, Gary M. & Dain C. Heer, DC, *Sex is Not a Four Letter Word But Relationship Often Times Is* (Kentucky: Lulu.com, 2011)

Douglas, Gary M. & Dain C. Heer, DC, *The Ten Keys to Total Freedom* (USA: Access Consciousness Publishing, 2012)

Gentry, Byron, DC with Mary Gentry, *Miracles of the Mind* (Florida: Rainbow Books, 1998)

Gladwell, Malcolm, *Blink* (New York: Little, Brown and Company, 2005)

Grattan, Brian, *Mahatma I & II* (Arizona: Light Technology Publishing, 1994)

Grayson, Henry, Ph.D. *Mindful Loving* (New York: Gotham Books, Penguin Group, 2003)

Hawkins, David R., MD, Ph.D., *Power vs. Force* (DVD: Arizona: Institute for Advanced Spiritual Research, 2005) (Book: Arizona: Verista Publishing, 2012, first published 1995)

Hay, Louise L., *Heal Your Body* (California: Hay House, Inc., 1982)

Heer, Dain C., DC, *Embodiment* (Kentucky: Lulu.com, 2013)

Hicks, Esther and Jerry, *The Astonishing Power of Emotions* (California: Hay House, Inc., 2007)

Hill, Napoleon, *Keys to Success* (New York: Plume, Penguin Group, 1994)

Hill, Napoleon, *Think & Grow Rich* (New York: Ballantine Books, 1937)

Holden, Robert, *Be Happy* (California: Hay House, Inc., 2009)

Holden, Robert, *Happiness Now!* (London: Hodder & Stoughton, 1998)

Holden, Robert, Ph.D., *Shift Happens* (California: Hay House, Inc., 2000)

Holmes, Ernest & Willis Kinnear, *Thoughts are Things* (Florida: Health Communications, Inc., 1967, 1999)

Hopcke, Robert H., *There are No Accidents,* (New York: Riverhead Books, 1997)

Hubbard, L. Ron, *Dianetics* (California: Bridge Publications, 1950, 2007)

Jeffers, Susan, *Life is Huge!* (London: Hodder & Stoughton, 2004)

Kamp, Jurriaan, *Turn Right for Enlightenment*, OdeWire(March-April 2012), p. 46–50

Katie, Byron, *Question Your Thinking*, Change the World (California: Hay House, Inc., 2007)

King, Deborah, *Truth Heals* (California: Hay House, 2009)

Langemeier, Loral, *YES! Energy* (California: Hay House, Inc., 2012)

Lee, Ilchi, *The Call of Sedona* (Arizona: Best Life Media, 2011)

Levenson, Lester, *No Attachments, No Aversions* (California: Lawrence Crane Enterprises, 2003)Bristol

Levenson, Lester, *The Power of Love* (California: Lawrence Crane Enterprises, Inc., 2006)

Levenson, Lester, *The Way to Complete Freedom* (California: Larry Crane Enterprises, Inc., 2003)

Lipton, Bruce H., Ph.D., *The Honeymoon Effect* (California: Hay House, Inc., 2013)

Mate, Gabor, M.D., *When the Body Says No* (New Jersey, John Wiley & Sons, 2003)

Matthews, Andrew, *Being Happy* (New York: Price, Stern, Sloan, Inc., Penguin Putnam Inc., 1988, 1990)

McKenna, Jed, *Spiritual Enlightenment* (Tennessee: Wisefool Press, 2010)

McKenna, Jed, *Spiritually Incorrect Enlightenment* (Tennessee: Wisefool Press, 2010)

McTaggart, Lynne, *The Intention Experiment* (New York: Free Press, Simon & Schuster, Inc., 2007)

Mollicone-Long, Gina, *Think or Sink* (New York: Sterling & Ross Publishers, 2010)

Murphy, Joseph, Ph.D., D.D., *The Power of Your Subconscious Mind* (New York, Reward Books, Prentice Hall, 2000, first published 1963) Myss, Myss, Myss, Caroline, *Why People Don't Heal* (Colorado: Sounds True Audios, 1994)

Peirce, Penney, *Frequency* (New York: Atria Books, Simon & Schuster, 2009)

Pert, Candace B., Ph.D., *Everything You Need to Know to Feel Go(o)d* (California: Hay House, Inc., 2006)

Phoenix, Jaden Rose, *Beyond Human* (Washington: Cherryhurst Press, Divine Life Technologies, LLC, 2011)

Ragnar, Peter, *The Awesome Science of Luck* (North Carolina: Roaring Lion Publishing, 2005)

Ray, James Arthur, *Practical Spirituality* (California: Sunark Press, 2003, 2005)

Ray, James Arthur, *The Science of Success* (California: Sunark Press, 2006)

Robbins, Mike, *Focus on the Good Stuff* (California: John Wiley & Sons, 2007)

Roman, Sanaya *Spiritual Growth* (California: H J Kramer, Inc., 1989)

Ruiz, Don Miguel, *The Four Agreements* (California: Amber-Allen Publishing, Inc., 1997)

Scheinfeld, Robert, *Busting Loose From The Money Game* (New Jersey, John Wiley & Sons, 2006)

Schwartz, David J., Ph.D., *The Magic of Thinking Big* (New York: Fireside, Simon & Schuster, 1959, 1965)

Shapiro, Rabbi Rami, *The Sacred Art of Lovingkindness* (Vermont: Skylight Paths Publishing, 2006)

Shimoff, Marci, *Happy for No Reason* (New York: Free Press, Simon & Schuster, Inc., 2008)

Truman, Karol K., *Feelings Buried Alive Never Die...* (Arizona: Olympus Distributing, 1991)

Walsh, Peter, *Does This Clutter Make My Butt Look Fat* (New York: Free Press, Simon & Schuster, 2008)

Waters, Owen, *The Shift* (Delaware: Infinite Being Publishing LLC, 2006)

Wilcock, David, *The Source Field Investigations* (New York, Dutton, Penguin Group, 2011)

Williams, Jr., Arthur L., *All You Can Do is All You Can Do But All You Can Do is Enough!* (New York: Ivy Books, Ballantine Books, 1988)

Womack, Womack, Belinda, *Angels Guide* (New York: Angels Guides Books, 1997)

Wright, Kurt, *Breaking the Rules* (Idaho: CPM Publishing, 1998)

Ziglar, Zig, *See You At The Top* (Louisiana: Pelican Publishing Co., 2005, first published 1975)

Zukav, Gary & Linda Francis, *The Mind of the Soul* (New York: Free Press, Simon & Schuster, 2003)